The Lost Cities of the Mayas

The life, art, and discoveries of Frederick Catherwood

Text by Fabio Bourbon

The gates to an enchanted treasure have closed once more. The flame in the temples has gone out. All is as it was before. Lost shadows and hollow-eyed ghosts drift through the deserted streets.
Miguel Angel Asturias

ARTES DE MEXICO

To my wife, Monica

Texts
Fabio Bourbon

Editorial Production
Valeria Manferto De Fabianis
Fabio Bourbon

Graphic design
Paola Piacco

ISBN 968-6533-89-3

10 9 8 7 6 5 4 3 2

Contents

*Pages 2-7—Plate XII,
depicting the ruins of Uxmal,
from* Views of Ancient
Monuments in Central
America, Chiapas and
Yucatan, *by Frederick
Catherwood*

Pages 3-6 – Uxmal: *Incidents of Travel in Yucatan*, by John L. Stephens.

PREFACE

One day in 1839, two intrepid explorers – one English, Frederick Catherwood, and the other American, John Lloyd Stephens – climbed the crumbling steps of the pyramids in the Mayan city of Copán. The pyramids had been overgrown by the jungle and their origins forgotten by the inhabitants of the region. The two were the first westerners to be aware of what was before them as they explored the immense terraces, the magnificent temples and the palaces that had been mysteriously abandoned centuries earlier. The city had been ignored by the Spanish conquistadors and had fallen into oblivion as it was slowly swallowed up by the luxuriant vegetation of the tropical forest. Human footsteps echoed once more between the crumbling walls of those extraordinary buildings as, filled with excitement, the pair studied inscriptions in an incomprehensible language, ran their hands over stone carvings and stuccoes created with superb workmanship and explored darkened rooms with the help of flickering oil lamps.

That episode in 1839 changed the lives of the two men and meant that the history of the civilizations of Central America had to be rewritten, for on that day, among the stelae raised by the ancient lords of Copán, the Maya came back to life.

Later, Stephens and Catherwood also discovered the ruins of Palenque, Uxmal, Chichén Itzá, Kabah, Sayil and many other cities overgrown by the forest. They brought to light the magnificent remains of a refined civilization that had inexplicably disappeared. Theirs was one of the most extraordinary archaeological adventures of all times and we shall journey through it with them thanks to the talent of Frederick Catherwood, the superb illustrator of the two travel diaries written by Stephens published in 1841 and 1843. For the first time, a selection of the more than two hundred engravings taken from the original drawings of the English artist have been collected in one volume and have been coloured by hand paying absolute faith to the text. In addition there is the reproduction of the whole of the very rare colour version of Views of Ancient Monuments in Central America, Chiapas and Yucatan, the portfolio of twenty six lithographs considered to be Catherwood's masterpiece.

The following pages describe the life of a man who was not just unusual in many ways but downright mysterious. As the reader will soon realize from this biography – which owes a great debt to the work of Victor Wolfgang von Hagen – the figure of Frederick

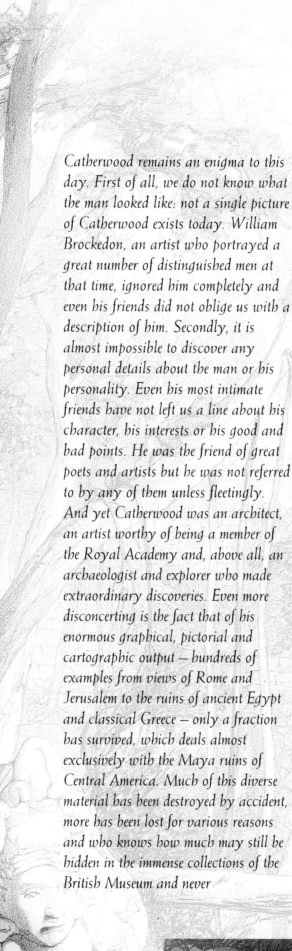

Catherwood remains an enigma to this day. First of all, we do not know what the man looked like: not a single picture of Catherwood exists today. William Brockedon, an artist who portrayed a great number of distinguished men at that time, ignored him completely and even his friends did not oblige us with a description of him. Secondly, it is almost impossible to discover any personal details about the man or his personality. Even his most intimate friends have not left us a line about his character, his interests or his good and bad points. He was the friend of great poets and artists but he was not referred to by any of them unless fleetingly. And yet Catherwood was an architect, an artist worthy of being a member of the Royal Academy and, above all, an archaeologist and explorer who made extraordinary discoveries. Even more disconcerting is the fact that of his enormous graphical, pictorial and cartographic output — hundreds of examples from views of Rome and Jerusalem to the ruins of ancient Egypt and classical Greece — only a fraction has survived, which deals almost exclusively with the Maya ruins of Central America. Much of this diverse material has been destroyed by accident, more has been lost for various reasons and who knows how much may still be hidden in the immense collections of the British Museum and never

systematically studied. Modest to excess, Catherwood did very little to bring himself to public notice or to recognize the value of his work (which, objectively speaking, was of great documentary importance); however, it is also true that several of his contemporaries may have been able to benefit from his pathological reserve. For example, unscrupulous editors almost certainly published numerous views taken from Catherwood's works which he sold for little money or lent to deceitful engravers who left off his name. The academic world of the time, as we shall see when discussing James Fergusson, was at least in part responsible for this calamitous diaspora: for reasons of envy, for fear of new ideas or for obtuse partisanship to the then current theories. It is also to be expected that his drawings came into the hands of private collectors who would have had no desire to publicize their purchases.

What has remained, however, is enough to show incontrovertibly that Frederick Catherwood was an exceptional documenter and an extraordinary artist. He had a spirit in which the flame of curiosity, knowledge and culture burnt bright. Despite its limitations, this book is a tribute to one of the major figures of the 19th century who inexplicably remained in the shadow until recent times and whose splendid work is almost unknown to the general public.

Fabio Bourbon

Page 8-9 – Plate II, depicting the ruins of Copán, from the standard edition of *Views of Ancient Monuments in Central America, Chiapas and Yucatan*, by Frederick Catherwood.

THE BIRTH OF MR. CATHERWOOD

Frederick Catherwood – or "Mr. Catherwood" as even his best friends called him all his life – was born on 27 February 1799 in Charles Square, Hoxton, a suburb of London.

An aura of romantic mystery surrounds this most extraordinary person since it is not even known what he looked like. Even though it seems nearly impossible, no picture of Catherwood has survived that can give us the faintest idea of his appearance. Despite fame and being known by a great number of celebrated artists of the period, it seems no-one ever drew or painted his portrait or even paid him, or us, the courtesy of providing a description of the man, however brief. The only, authentic self-portrait that Catherwood executed was inserted in one of his canvasses (the Panorama of Jerusalem) which has inauspiciously disappeared. John Lloyd Stephens, who was his intimate friend for fifteen years and who shared all types of adventure with him in the wilds of Central America, only speaks of him as "Mr. Catherwood" in his extensive diaries of their journeys together which were published in 1841 and 1843. Of Catherwood, there remains only this unusual epithet, so

18th century in its scrupulous formality, and a tiny figure that appears in a lithograph taken from his masterpiece, Views of Ancient Monuments in Central America, Chiapas and Yucatan, which has consigned his name and art to posterity. Catherwood is shown as a 40-year-old man of average build, with straight, long fair hair, wearing white trousers, a beige frock-coat and a crumpled white hat. In truth, much of the responsibility for the man's disconcerting anonymity is due to Frederick Catherwood himself, whose modesty could even have been pathological.

The first symptoms of this extreme reserve became evident during his infancy but increased to excess as an adult. He was always cautious, rather formal, and tended to belittle himself. Often he would indulge in periods of complete silence or, to use a term that was beloved by doctors of the age, he fell subject to "bouts of melancholy". Nevertheless, he had an agile and brilliant intellect and was endowed with an inexhaustible enthusiasm and interior strength which were able to balance this pernicious form of depression and sustain him in difficult moments

during his adventurous explorations of far-off lands. Nor do we know anything of his personality. A biography of Catherwood is therefore necessarily tied to mere objective data gathered from the few official documents and from the writings of those who knew him. These revolve essentially around his scholastic career, artistic experience and celebrated travels. What the passions were that moved his heart, what his tastes were, his qualities and faults, all these must remain relegated to the plan of pure inference.

Unfortunately, we do not even know about his family or his early years. Certainly his parents were well-off though they were not members of the aristocracy. His father, Nathaniel, had Scottish origins: the name Catherwood seems to be derived from a river near Edinburgh, the Calder. The family of his mother, Elizabeth, had an Irish background. Of Alfred, Frederick's only brother, born in 1803, it is only known that he graduated in medicine at the University of Glasgow, that he practised at the London Dispensary from 1842, that he published a treatise on pathologies of the lungs and that he died in 1865.

Pages 10-11 – In plate XXIV of *Views of Ancient Monuments in Central America, Chiapas and Yucatan* appears the only known image of Frederick Catherwood (to the right).

INFANCY

In the early years of the 19th century, Charles Square was surrounded by lovely houses built in the second half of the previous century. It was still a quiet and elegant corner that had been left untouched by the proliferation of workshops and laboratories that had sprung up around. It was described at the time as a square looked onto by houses of "highly respectable" families. Young Frederick grew up in this well-to-do neighbourhood and received his first education at the nearby Haberdasher's School, one of the many family-run institutes of the period. To fully understand Catherwood's good fortune, we must consider that at the start of the century only the children of the nobility automatically enjoyed a standard education at a renowned college. Entrance to a school of a son of a bourgeois family even slightly less well-off than the Catherwoods was completely unthinkable. Frederick remained at Haberdasher's until the end of the eighth year studying Linguistic Morphology and Grammar. He must have been a gifted pupil to judge by the diploma he received, on which was written, "a good grammarian, fluent orator and poet, well versed in the knowledge of Latin, Greek and Hebrew". Undoubtedly, he had received a suitable all round training since, in the years to come, Frederick was to show himself a competent linguist, able to speak Greek, Italian and Arabic correctly and to read Hebrew.

Moreover, his knowledge of mathematics and geometry was suitably deep to facilitate later studies of architecture. From the little information that has reached us, it seems that the natural artistic talent of the young Frederick showed itself at an early age and was encouraged by his parents. It is not surprising, therefore, that despite his brilliant studies in the Arts, his real interests lay elsewhere.

During this period London was

becoming the new "capital of the world". The city was in continual expansion, a megalopolis where new and larger buildings were built every day. It was probably during afternoons spent with his inseparable friend, Joseph Severn, wandering around the city excitedly observing the unending rows of large buildings, that the seed of his most ardent passion was sown. Or maybe it was his friend Joseph, four years older and apprentice in the workshop of the engraver

William Bond, who set off the interest for design and architecture in Frederick's young and avid mind. It is certain that he had hardly turned sixteen when he left school to be presented to Michael Meredith, an architect of some standing who had exhibited his drawings at the Royal Academy. It was 1815: Frederick signed a contract as an apprentice which obliged him to work for the studio for five years. It was to be an eventful period that was crucial to the training of the young artist.

Pages 12-13 – A view of London in the early nineteenth century; on the right is the Custom House.

Page 13 top – Another view of London: this lithograph shows the Post Office building.

Page 13 bottom – View of London in the early nineteenth century.

YOUTH AND STUDIES

Books illustrated with architectural views of the most important buildings in certain regions or countries were fairly popular in the first decades of the 19th century. A famous example are the various editions of the Jennings' Landscape Annual *that showed lithographs of the drawings of Spain made by David Roberts, one of the most appreciated English landscape artists of the century. Michael Meredith also subscribed to this trend which was a good source of income to the artists. It was therefore to accompany his employer on a long trip across England in search of attractive views that Catherwood left his family home for the first time in his life. The experience without doubt filled Frederick with enthusiasm and it helped him to learn the fundamental*

notions of technical drawing: from the use of a square to the rules of perspective. The years that followed saw the inexpert boy become a mature and professional artist with a sure hand and good intuition for composition. His salary was meagre and the study routine often boring but Frederick had a strong character and was determined to learn everything that Meredith was able to teach him. As the number of his sketches continued to increase, the young man discovered he had a true talent though heavily influenced by the aesthetic tastes then in vogue, decadent Romanticism and severe Classicism, the two antagonists in an eternal polemic on the meaning of beauty. This was the era of Turner, Constable, Walpole, Holland, Martin and a plethora of

minor artists that willingly gratified – or instigated – the maudlin tastes of the aristocratic London ladies and their no less sensitive husbands. The neo-Gothic style flourished wildly but was met blow for blow by the austerity of John Nash and the Neoclassicism of Sir John Soane. The rise of an accentuated interest in the world of the bizarre and the occult on the one hand was mitigated by the return to the precision and propriety of the Classicists on the other. Catherwood remained between the two and in some way attempted to synthesize them in a language of his own. In doing so, he showed he possessed a critical sense and balanced attitude that were greater than one might expect in so young an individual. When his five years training were up and he

Pages 14-15 – One of the symbols of Georgian London: the Quadrant with a view of Regent Street.

Page 14 top – Another view of early nineteenth-century London: the Coliseum, at Regent's Park.

Page 14 bottom – The Royal Exchange, an excellent example of the Neoclassical style in vogue during Frederick Catherwood's youth.

realised that his employer had no more to teach him, Frederick left Meredith's office and prepared to organize the first public exhibition of his own works, but his friend since childhood, Joseph Severn, altered Catherwood's life. Severn had achieved no little fame himself in the meantime having just been awarded the Gold Medal for artistic merit by the Royal Academy. Severn was still as he had been – a good-humoured, open and cordial young man – but his professional reputation was already so great that he had been welcomed as part of the artistic coterie that gravitated around the celebrated journalist James Henry Leigh Hunt. Leigh Hunt had published the Romantic genius of John Keats in his weekly journal, The Examiner, and shown himself strongly hostile to Byron; so it was not by chance that around 1820 Severn figured as an assiduous visitor of the young poet whose health was already threatened by consumption. It was through Severn, therefore, that Catherwood was introduced to what was for him a completely new and fascinating world and it is sure that he came to know both the authoritative journalist and the diaphanous poet. Moreover, good mentor that he was, Severn warmly suggested that his friend should continue his studies so that the artistic talent that Severn had already noticed might bear fruit. Catherwood recognized the value of this suggestion and enrolled in the free art courses at the Royal Academy. This celebrated institution had been founded in 1766 by John Reynolds with the name of "Society of Artists of Great Britain" but this had been altered two years later. Famous artists taught students able to demonstrate particular talents. In 1820, once he had passed the entrance examination, Catherwood had the privilege of attending the drawing courses given by Johann Heinrich Füssli – an artist of Swiss origin who was one of the great initiators of Romanticism – and lessons on perspective by William Turner, one of the greatest English painters of the 19th century. Yet, however much these two fascinated Catherwood, it was Sir John Soane that he was most influenced by who at the time was professor of architecture at the Academy. At seventy seven years of age, Soane was one of the greatest British exponents of Neoclassicism. He had written many treatises on its principles and, besides the famous Bank of England, had designed Marylebone church, the Ministry of Public Works and many other buildings. Weaned on the scientific and philosophic rationalism of the 17th century, Soane had reinforced the classical and Vitruvian current of thought, taking it as far as practical limits would allow in his continual search for formal purity that sharply contrasted with the tendencies of the late Baroque. Small and delicate, Sir John was a brilliant man with a contagious enthusiasm and the rare gift of being able to enthral his listeners with his eloquence, so it is easy to understand why his lessons were so popular among the students of the Royal Academy. Frederick was a true enthusiast. The words of the professor forced him to

Page 16 top – Portrait of Heinrich Füssli (1741 - 1825). Born in Switzerland, he soon moved to London. A painter, art critic and teacher, he is considered one of the masters of the early Romanticism.

reflect on the laws of geometry, the authenticity of elementary forms and the necessity of purifying architecture of everything superfluous. Soane, who had travelled extensively in Italy and Greece as a young man, was inspired by the formal canons of classical antiquity while his ideals of clarity and balance were related to universal laws and aimed at serving a rigorous and enlightened rationalism. As well as teaching the golden rules of architecture, he never ceased to emphasize the importance of painting and sculpture. He believed that to be a complete artist, a good architect had to know how to draw the human

figure correctly. While Frederick avidly absorbed the teachings of Sir John, he discovered the splendour of the architecture of ancient Rome through the work of Giovanni Battista Piranesi whom Soane greatly admired. It is true to say that it was through contact with the work of the Italian architect and engraver – Piranesi's visionary interpretations of the past, his dramatic and complex compositions using the effects of perspective and chiaroscuro – that a passion for archaeology, landscape art and architectural caprice was ignited in Frederick. His vocation was by then almost decided and it burned more intensely day by day.

Undoubtedly, the influences of Soane and Piranesi were the determining factors for the rest of his career. Enchanted by the series of engravings made by Piranesi in 1761 entitled De Romanorum magnificentia et architectura that Sir John used to show his students during the lessons, Frederick applied himself to working on views of archaeological subjects. One of these was displayed to approval at the Royal Academy so legitimizing the young artist's aspirations. Catherwood's most ardent wish now was to travel in order to deepen his knowledge and to find new inspirations for the creative force that animated him. But fate

Pages 16-17 – The University of London in a print of the early decades of the nineteenth century. Catherwood could not afford university, but attended the courses of the Royal Academy.

Page 17 top – Portrait of Sir John Soane (1753-1837). One of the leading exponents of the Neoclassical English architecture, with his enthralling lessons at the Royal Academy he notably influenced Catherwood's artistic taste.

Page 17 bottom – Another important source of inspiration for Catherwood was the work of Giovanni Battista Piranesi, the famous Italian engraver and architect. In particular *De Romanorum magnificentia et architectura*, from which this view of the Roman Forum is taken.

took a hand in the shape of an unexpected event that had nothing to do with the academic world. The health of John Keats was rapidly worsening and, in September 1820, his friends had decided to send him to Rome in the hope that the mild climate of the Eternal City might bring some improvement. John Severn offered to accompany him, his only income being a study leave of one year in Rome paid by the Royal Academy. When Catherwood said goodbye to them at the port of London, Severn made Frederick promise that as soon as his studies ended, he would come to Rome.

HIS FIRST TRAVELS

The chance to see Severn came more quickly than expected as, unfortunately, Keats died on the 23rd February 1821 overwhelmed by hereditary consumption. Overcome with sorrow, Severn fell into deep depression and wrote to Frederick asking him to come to Rome as early as possible to relieve his spirits. And so it was on the 14th September 1821 that "Mr Catherwood" finally reached the Eternal City where he was enthusiastically welcomed by his old friend. Once installed in the convenient apartment Severn had found for them

both in Via San Isidoro, Frederick was introduced to the circle of English artists living in the city. There were twenty or so of them who met in the Society of Englishmen. Among them were Thomas Leverton Donaldson, Joseph Bonomi, Henry Parke and Joseph Scoles, all of whom Catherwood would be close to for a long time. Scoles in particular was a friend for life and it is to him that we owe the few but useful biographical notes on Catherwood. Frederick was enthused and astonished by the Roman monuments and dedicated himself to studies of classical architecture with renewed ardour. During the first few decades of the 19th century, Rome and its landscapes were one of the most inspirational motifs of European painting and art: there are clear echoes in the work of Ingres, Corot, Eckersberg and Géricault to name but a few. Nor could "Mr Catherwood" remain unaffected by the Forum, the Colosseum, the Pantheon or the other major monuments and he gave himself wholeheartedly to exploring the city and its infinite treasures. Rome was in a fervour of "studies of antiquities" following enthusiasm for the Neoclassical and the ambitious Napoleonic programme pursued by Pope Pius VII that together gave rise to an era of exploration and excavation. The young English artist was therefore able to admire the recently unearthed ruins of Trajan's Forum and the Roman Forum

Pages 18 top, 19 centre and bottom – The Roman Forum, the Colosseum and the Pantheon in the engravings by Luigi Rossini, 1829

Page 18 bottom – St. Peter's, in Rome, in a print made at the time of Catherwood's sojourn.

Page 19 top – This splendid view of the Roman Forum is by David Roberts, who executed it in 1859, six years after his visit to the Eternal City. The famous landscape artist of Scottish origin almost certainly met Catherwood, but no written record has survived of this encouter.

under the guidance of the brilliant Thomas Donaldson, the member of the group that had been in Rome for the longest time and who willingly acted as guide. Just as it was a chosen place for poets and artists, Rome was also the gilded refuge for many rich bon vivants from all over Europe; the offspring of good families, aristocrats looking for cultural excitement, lords and ladies taken by archaeology, and artists of various levels of brilliancy amongst which shone Canova, Thorvaldsen and Gibson. A few months after his arrival, Frederick had become a frequenter of this refined and heterogeneous company to which he had been presented, of course, by Severn. Not that Joseph was completely disinterested in doing so as

for some time he had been pursued by the wealthy, cultured and lovely Lady Westmoreland, the uninhibited wife of the elderly Duke of Westmoreland. It was in order to release himself from this situation that Severn had thought to offer her the unprepared Catherwood. As soon as Frederick had recovered his breath after laying eyes on the rich, sparkling, beautiful, blonde Jane, he had no cause for complaint. On the contrary, he quickly accepted the offer that Severn had tried to avoid, that of following the aristocrat, who had become infatuated with ancient Egypt following the amazing discoveries made by Belzoni, on a long expedition down the Nile. Besides being frightened by the attentions of a married, high-placed and

published in the Dictionary of Architecture. *This can be considered the first official archaeological work carried out by Catherwood. Later, in the summer of 1822, still fired by an insatiable thirst for knowledge, Frederick made several journeys through the south of Italy where he had his first encounters with Greek architecture. Bewitched by the ancient theatre at Taormina set against the majestic mass of Mount Etna, he painted a large landscape in oils which was subsequently exhibited in America with great success and bought for a private collection in New York. Accompanied by Parke and Scoles, in the autumn Catherwood set sail for Greece where they landed just as the struggle for independence against the Turks was beginning. To some*

heroic spirit but by a real passion for classical antiquities and yet, at the bottom of their sudden decision, there must have been a spirit of daring or simply pure ignorance of the situation. As it was, they did not run any serious risks and their love of adventure had to be satisfied by the weeks they remained blocked in Athens by the siege of the Turkish troops. In the shadow of the Acropolis, the three young Englishmen found the time to further appreciate the sublime canons of Phidias that they must have begun to study in London when contemplating the marble decorations of the Parthenon, held in the British Museum since 1806 thanks to the enterprise of Lord Elgin.

Unfortunately, besides not knowing the exact route the three friends followed

utterly fickle woman, Severn wished to conclude a painting he had started some time before as his examination subject for the Royal Academy. To his merit, it should be added that as the tender but completely unexpected friendship between Catherwood and the irrepressible Lady Westmoreland developed, Severn began to worry not a little. In December 1821, a few weeks after their first meeting, the impeccable "Mr Catherwood" had become Lady Westmoreland's lover and been transferred lock, stock and barrel into her luxurious villa. The remove had occurred with Severn's permission though by then he was feeling very guilty about the whole affair. However, the affair came to a rapid and furious head and the ménage broke up leaving in Catherwood the single burning desire to finally visit Egypt.

In the meantime, though, he had accepted the task of drawing whatever the Duchess of Devonshire unearthed during the excavations she financed in the Roman Forum. Also involved in this interesting work of documentation was Catherwood's friend Henry Parke and their drawings showing the local antiquities and catacombs were

extent the liberal spirit that was pervading public opinion and the artistic and literary society of half Europe contributed to this decision. Indeed, while the governments of the great conservative powers showed themselves openly hostile to the revolution, societies inspired by the cultural and political ideals of Romanticism supported the Greeks, had collected arms and money for the cause and men had volunteered to fight with the Greeks from every nation. The three architects were not moved by such a

while on the Greek peninsula, we have not even been left one of the drawings Catherwood undertook during those long months. We only know that their stay in Greece was protracted much longer than expected and that the three did not leave Athens until 1824 when they found an escape route towards Syria and the Levant by way of the Greek islands. As the winds of war were blowing throughout the entire region, "Mr Catherwood" and his friends had no choice but to seek refuge in the only safe haven for English fugitives, Egypt.

THE YEARS IN EGYPT

Following the Napoleonic expedition and the extraordinary deeds of adventurers like Belzoni - the Italian who had violated the pyramids' secret, removed the sand from the entrance to the temple at Abu Simbel and discovered the tomb of Sethi I - an insatiable curiosity for anything related to the ancient land of the Pharaohs grew in Europe. Egypt was governed by Pasha Mohammed Alì, who had risen to power in 1805 after chasing out the Turks, and was a land full of uncertainties, meaning that western travellers ran up against problems of every sort. In spring 1824, Catherwood, Parke and Scoles hired a boat, emptied it of rats by sinking it to the bottom of a canal for a few days, and took off up the Nile. On the adventurous journey that took them beyond the First Cataract and into Nubian territory, the three young men mapped and drew all the principal monuments they came across so that they became the first authentic pioneers of Egyptian archaeology. On their return to Alexandria in October 1825, Frederick came into contact with a young English nobleman, Robert Hay of Linplum. Archaeologist, draftsman and antique collector, this unusual young man was later to fit out an expedition of draftsmen, cartographers and "antiquarians" that sailed up the Nile

as far as Nubia to study in depth all the known sites and others not yet made public. Some of the members of this mixed and brilliant company were James Haliburton, John Gardner Wilkinson, George Hoskins, Francis Arundale, Edward Lane and an old friend of Frederick's, Joseph Bonomi: all names that were to go down in the history of Egyptology. Indeed, it was Bonomi and Arundale that were responsible for the cataloguing and illustrations of many collections of pharaonic antiquities, some of which belonged to the British Museum and were published between 1843-45 under the title Gallery of Egyptian Antiquities Selected from the British Museum. Hay was very impressed by the descriptions of the Egyptian monuments and by the series of drawings he was shown, to the extent that he would willingly have enlisted Frederick on the spot but all those years of wandering had exhausted Catherwood's finances and he felt nostalgic for England. He boarded a boat at Alexandria and went first to

Athens to collect all those things he had been obliged to leave during the siege. He then sailed to Rome where he stopped off for a few days to stay with his friend Joseph Severn who, as always, welcomed him with open arms.

He finally arrived in London in January 1826 after four and a half

Rob.ᵗ Hay

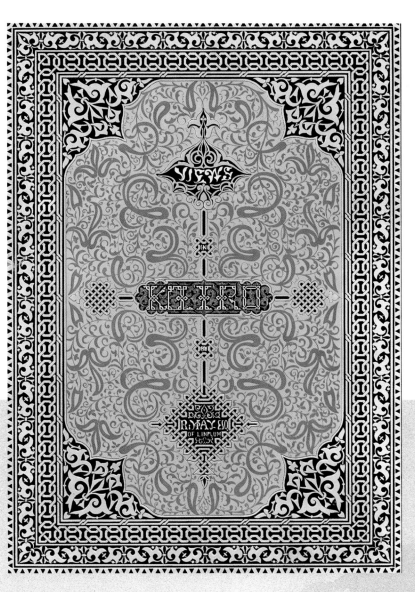

Page 22 left – Robert Hay (1799-1855) is shown dressed as a Turk in a daguerrotype.

Page 22, 23 – This view of the Nubian temple of Gerf Hussein was drawn by Catherwood in 1824 during his first trip down the Nile.

Page 23 top – The frontispiece of "Views in Cairo", published by Robert Hay in 1840.

years away. England was in that period undergoing great change and consequently social and economic tension. The Industrial Revolution was radically changing the country and against this difficult background, Catherwood tried to practise his profession as architect but with little luck. As usual, the information available on this period of his life is fragmentary and lacking in detail but it is known he designed several labourers' cottages and a large conservatory. No doubt he also had other commissions but not enough to support him. To put his finances back in order he sold some of the drawings he had made on the banks of the Nile and, feeling sure of the public's interest, he exhibited a number of illustrations at the Royal Academy, but even this initiative must have met with little success as, at the end of that

year, he packed his bags in an instant and embarked once more for Egypt as soon as he received a letter from Robert Hay asking Frederick to join his expedition up the Nile.

After spending a few more days with Severn in Rome, Catherwood returned to Alexandria in 1829. It is a great misfortune that, with the exception of a few scribbled letters, this singular person did not leave any written description of his voyage which might be compared to those of other artists and explorers of the age. For example, ten years later, David Roberts described the huge city with evident emotion. "Alexandria was right in front of us, with mosques and palm-trees that gave it a different atmosphere from any I had ever breathed before . . . The bay was crowded with a large number of vessels, many of which were warships; our boat

was soon surrounded by the most picturesque boatmen I have ever seen". Consequently, we are obliged to fill out Catherwood's conciseness with a little imagination of our own. The large port city was an indescribable confusion of sumptuously dressed gentlemen, naked black slaves, deafening camel drivers, Greek and Jewish merchants and people of every nationality that headed this way and that without any particular destination. Yet, notwithstanding the remains of its glorious past, greater interest was to be found in the streets of Cairo where the members of Robert Hay's group, who were studying the pyramids at Giza, met frequently. Catherwood's first task was to measure the dimensions and draw to scale the huge and eternal abodes of Cheops, Chephren and Mycerinus. The result of the expedition was forty nine large-folio

Page 24 – The temple of Wadi Sabua in Nubia drawn by Catherwood in 1824.

Pages 24, 25 – This splendid view of Abu Simbel in Nubia was also drawn by Catherwood during the 1824 expedition. Note that the entrance to the hypogeum rooms cleared of sand by Giovanni Battista Belzoni in 1817 was blocked once more.

volumes furnished with hundreds of pictures that Hay gave to the British Museum in 1879 where they are still kept. Strange though it may seem, Hay only found the time to publish one book during his lifetime, called Views in Cairo which was published in London in 1840. This volume contains just one of Catherwood's views of the Pyramids which consequently became one of the few works (with the exception of the illustrations of the Maya remains) that his contemporaries were able to admire. All the rest of his massive amount of documentation was either lost or is still kept in the Hay collection. About thirty years ago, the scholar Victor Wolfgang von Hagen managed to discover some of the original illustrations among the enormous quantity of paper and to attribute them correctly. This heavy task was made

all the more burdensome by the fact that the reluctant "Mr Catherwood" had the terrible habit of not signing his drawings (or at most scribbling "FC" in the corner). Other sketches were later found in the same collection by other scholars but even today no definitive catalogue exists.

Frederick tackled his work with the same meticulousness and calligraphic precision of the ancient copyists but also shared with them the rule of silence and modesty. It is easy to imagine him sitting under the boiling sun completely absorbed in his work; a solitary and inscrutable figure even to his own companions. It is highly indicative that in the nearly five years that he and his colleagues were intent on their study of the Egyptian monuments, not a single word was written about his character. No witty remark or anecdote that

throws some light on his character has come down to us. The only fact we have is that he owned an extremely modern, seven round revolver (Colt only patented their first revolver in 1835) that greatly impressed the local people and was known throughout the Nile valley.

Once the expedition had finished studying the archaeological area of Giza, it moved camp to the ruins of Memphis. This used to be the capital of pharaonic Egypt during the Old Kingdom and is located near the sites of Sakkarah, Abusir, Meidum and Dashur. Here stand the famous Step Pyramid built by King Djoser, the Red Pyramid and the Rhomboidal Pyramid. When they had explored these monuments, the group moved south to Beni Hassan, Abydos and Dendera. By the end of summer 1832, Hay's expedition had arrived at the majestic ruins of ancient Thebes, the capital of Egypt during the Middle and New Kingdoms. The city of Thebes was located where the villages and temples of Luxor and Karnak now stand.

Catherwood spent September surveying the entire archaeological site

and produced a detailed map with the ground plans of all the main buildings. He also drew the obelisks of the temple of Luxor, different views of the Ramesseum, and the interior of the tomb of Ramses IV with its enormous sarcophagus in the Valley of the Kings. Hay established the camp inside this sepulchre where it was cool and well-ventilated. Two views of the tomb of Sethi I, one of the tomb of Ramses III and a panorama of the entire valley can perhaps be ascribed to Catherwood. In the meantime, Arundale drew the two large sacred complexes of Karnak and Luxor and Bonomi reproduced as many hieroglyphics as possible plus wall paintings in the tombs so far discovered in the Valleys of the Kings and Queens.

In October, Catherwood accompanied another member of the expedition, George Hoskins, to the oasis of Kharga in the desert towards Libya. At the end of 1832, Frederick and James Haliburton began to measure and draw the Colossi of Memnon, the two immense statues erected by Amenhotep III in front of his own memorial temple of which only ruins now remain. To do so, he built scaffolding around them and

measured every single element. His illustrations were the first to have been made with scientific accuracy and are still kept as part of the Hay collection. Catherwood made use of a "camera lucida" or light chamber to help him sketch the outline of an object on a piece of paper. The instrument had been invented some years before by William Wollaston and consisted of a four-sided

Page 27 – Portrait of Mohammed Ali, pasha of Egypt from 1805-49.

prism on a stand over the drawing paper.

The expedition progressed south from Thebes stopping at Hermonthis, Esna, Edfu, Kom Ombo, Elephantine and, finally, on the wonderful island of Philae, just upstream of the First Cataract. In the weeks spent among the colonnades of the sanctuary consecrated to Isis, the untiring Catherwood continued to pile up an enormous amount of material, today mostly untraceable. Of all the illustrations carried out on the island of Philae, he kept for himself only a watercolour of the great temple by moonlight which was exhibited in New York in 1845. From the island in the river, Hay wanted to go on into Nubia to continue the work on the great Egyptian monuments to be found along the fertile banks of the Nile. These included the extraordinary temples that were to be

removed from their original sites when the High Dam of Aswan was built and removed to a safe location above the waters of the growing Lake Nasser.

After a few weeks spent with the rest of the expedition, Frederick decided to return to Cairo with Francis Arundale bringing to a close an adventure of epic proportions. Although it was completely fresh in his mind, he went against the grain of the times, and published no writings or drawings of his experiences nor did he attempt to

gain notoriety or glory for himself in any way. This certainly was there for the taking in an era that was so avid for exotic images, but his choice is not so strange given his peculiar attitude to publicity. Practically all his companions, however, soon brought out publications of one sort or another detailing their extraordinary experience. Haliburton, in particular, left the British Museum seventy seven volumes, for the most part unpublished, including his travel diary, archaeological notes and a large number of drawings. It is probable that, in the midst of those by the author, there are also a number by Catherwood.

Once he reached Cairo, Frederick found a way to offer his services to the highest authority in Egypt, Pasha Mohammed Alì himself. For a while, Catherwood gave lessons in architecture at the Islamic university of al-Azhar while also surveying and restoring Cairo mosques. In doing so, he built up enormous experience in this field. Then, armed with a decree issued by the

Pasha, he had occasion to visit Tunisia which was then a vassal state of Egypt. Here he was able to explore Dougga, the ancient Thugga, which was one of the best preserved Roman cities in Africa Proconsularis. While in Dougga he drew a splendid Roman funerary monument which was later destroyed. Strangely, Frederick wrote a detailed account of this visit which he published in New York in 1845. It is probable that during this trip, he travelled on till he reached the ruins of Carthage (near modern day Tunis) and Algiers as many years later he exhibited some large "panoramas" in New York that included some of these two places.

Pages 27, 28 – This drawing by Catherwood shows the tip of an obelisk and a detail of the Colossi of Memnon. It was inserted by John Stephens in his book "Incidents of Travel in Central America, Chiapas and Yucatan" to show how different Mayan art was to Egyptian art.

Page 28 – Two views of the Colossi of Memnon by Catherwood for Robert Hay in 1832.

Page 28 – The Mosque of Omar in Jerusalem drawn by William Henry Bartlett.

Page 29 top – The Pool of Hezekiah, in Jerusalem, in a lithograph by William Henry Bartlett published, like the previous illustration, in *Walks about the City and Environs of Jerusalem* (1844).

Page 29 centre – A lithograph by Bartlett showing the Mount of Olives in Jerusalem seen from the walls.

provisions for the forthcoming trip to the Holy Land. He is a young man of few words but confident in his manner; he is perfectly at ease in the throng as he wanders among the market stalls loaded with nameless goods, smelling the aroma wafting from the spices, against the continual background hubbub from the crowded cafés.

Aided in their venture by nine camels, the three colleagues left for Suez dressed in local clothing to attract less attention. They followed the ancient caravan route to St. Catherine's

more certain considering that this mosque, built around 699 by Caliph Abd al-Malik, has always been one of Islam's holiest sites. The splendid golden dome covers Abraham's Rock where a footprint, according to tradition, marks where Mohammed ascended to heaven. Amazingly, this is one of Catherwood's few adventures that was described in his own hand; he did so in a letter written to an old friend, William Bartlett, a traveller and English writer, that Bartlett published in 1844 in his book Walks about the City and Environs

Frederick's enthusiasm did not diminish in any way, nor did his vocation as an explorer, and so, having completed his work for Mohammed Alì, he left for Arabia Petrea on 29 August 1833 with Bonomi and Arundale. It is from the memoirs of this trip that we are able to learn something of the mysterious "Mr Catherwood". After his years of living in Egypt, he had adopted local dress including a turban. He spoke Arabic fluently and had also adapted his manner and behaviour to those of the Middle East. In the eyes of his companions, he even seemed to have lost some of his natural reserve. We can try to imagine him, his face darkened by the sun, as he winds his way through a bazaar, intent on negotiating good prices for water flasks, blankets and

monastery in the Sinai where they stayed long enough to climb the peak of Mount Sinai. Then they continued towards Gaza and finally Jerusalem which they reached on 6 October. Once they arrived in the Holy City, helped by the decree issued by the Pasha of Egypt, Frederick had the opportunity to put together some extraordinary documentation. Showing uncommon determination and courage, he became the first "infidel" to set foot in the fabulous and splendid Omar Mosque. He spent some days beforehand sketching the exterior of the mosque, then, on 13 November 1833, dressed as an Egyptian official, he could not resist the temptation to draw the interior. At the time, such a transgression was paid for with one's life, and this was all the

of Jerusalem. Frederick, with only an assistant for company, entered the mosque, set up his equipment, sat down and started to draw while a crowd of two hundred of the faithful, at first amazed by the apparition, became ever more hostile: "A few moments more and they would have pulled us to pieces", he wrote. He was saved by the providential arrival of the governor of Jerusalem with whom he was on good terms and to whom he explained that he was there on the Pasha's orders in order to organise restoration of the holy building. The governor was duped by the story and placated the crowd; he then gave Frederick six weeks to complete the work. Subsequently, Catherwood exploited the opportunity to take the astonished Bonomi and

Arundale into the building with him. When it became known that the Pasha was about to arrive in the city, Frederick decided it was time for a change of scenery. In the two months he had spent in Jerusalem, he had produced an exceptional amount of work. Using his faithful light chamber, he had designed a panoramic view of the entire city which some years later was to provide him with some income, although in an unexpected way. He had also produced a detailed map of the city which was printed in 1835 on his return to London and which one day was to be bought by a certain John Stephens.

abandoned at the time of the Crusades and was still abandoned in 1834 when the trio arrived. Gerasa was a superb expanse of monumental ruins centring on the huge and entirely colonnaded Greek forum. Ecstatic at the beauty of the place, Catherwood was the first to produce a detailed site map which is today held at the British Museum. Unfortunately, their visit was not problem-free as the local Bedouins were rather hostile and Frederick was obliged to put on a show of force and fire his famous revolver in the air. To complicate matters further, Arundale's health worsened with an unexpected

bout of epilepsy. It could not have been easy to work under such conditions but "Mr Catherwood" was not one to give in easily and, in fact, he wanted to continue to Baalbek in Lebanon, accompanied this time only by Arundale who despite his poor health must have been an obstinate sort too. Once they reached Baalbek, the ancient city of Heliopolis, Catherwood worked intensively. He drew the massive remains of the Temple of Jupiter, the Temple of Bacchus and the small and elegant temple dedicated to Venus. The two spent a good part of March in Damascus, of which Frederick drew a panoramic view, and then they continued to Palmyra, the fabulous city in the Syrian desert which became a Roman colony in 183 AD. Today it is known as one of the most spectacular archaeological sites in the Middle East. "Mr Catherwood" left Palmyra in April 1834 and headed for Beirut where he took ship for Alexandria before going on to England.

Satisfied with his achievements in the Holy City, Frederick was restless to visit other places. He convinced Arundale to follow him on this new venture. They set off for Gerasa, situated in what is today Jordan. The city was essentially Hellenistic before being taken over by the Romans and underwent a period of great prosperity from about 50 AD as a result of the caravan trade. It was completely

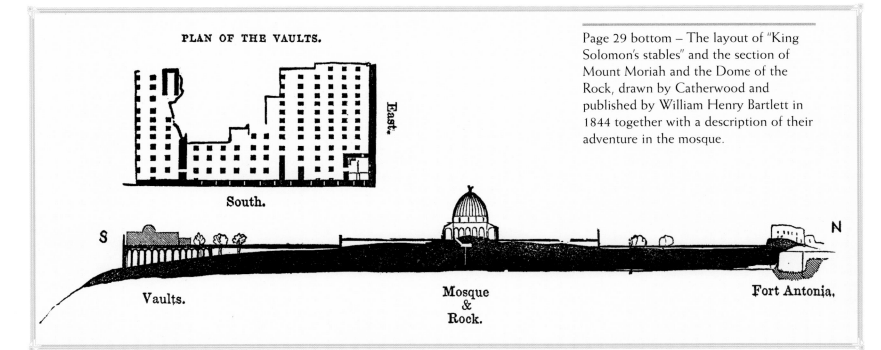

PLAN OF THE VAULTS.

East.

South.

S   N

Vaults.   Mosque & Rock.   Fort Antonia.

Page 29 bottom – The layout of "King Solomon's stables" and the section of Mount Moriah and the Dome of the Rock, drawn by Catherwood and published by William Henry Bartlett in 1844 together with a description of their adventure in the mosque.

Pages 30, 31 – The large rotonda in Leicester Square in London in which Catherwood displayed his celebrated "panoramas".

Page 31 – A view of London with Westminster Bridge and Westminster Abbey in a print of the early 1800's.

Back in London in 1835, after years of wandering and research, Frederick had considerable professional resources to offer but few financial means. To make a living, he became a landscape painter in the employ of Robert Burford in Leicester Square. This new profession had nothing to do with his archaeological work in the Middle East but, if nothing else, he was able to put his technical experience to good use. The United Kingdom in those years was heading for an age of unequalled prosperity. William IV was at the end of his controversial reign and soon the young Victoria was to create an empire of extraordinary size. The population hungered after anything that was new, they wanted to know about far-off places and to widen their horizons and clever entrepreneurs had found just the solution to satisfy these desires: anyone with just a few pennies in his pocket could travel, metaphorically speaking, to distant

invention, the name of which ended up describing the building the paintings were shown in, was attributed to the Irish painter Robert Barker. He had called it a cyclorama when he presented it to the public for the first time in Edinburgh in 1788. It met with enormous success and was brought to London five years later under the patronage of Sir Joshua Reynolds. In a short time, Barker's invention was copied by a great number of entrepreneurs and large circular buildings sprang up in all the large cities where the crowd could admire views of distant cities, be present at coronations or battles, or simply marvel at the beauty of sunsets in exotic places. The most far-sighted of the many emulators of the ingenious Irish painter was without doubt Robert Burford who bought the large Panorama in Leicester Square in 1826, the most famous of all. Burford was also a good painter and had been responsible for many of the enormous canvases exhibited by Barker, but by 1835 he was an able businessman and

he was on the perennial lookout for artists that had recently returned from abroad. Catherwood, fresh from his journeys in the Middle East, was exactly what he wanted. As for Frederick, he had had no success in finding a publisher for his drawings, not even the extraordinary documentation of Omar's Mosque in Jerusalem, and was in urgent need of cash. Consequently, he allowed his drawings to be used to create a "Panorama of Jerusalem" on which he was to paint the architectural details himself.

Actually, Catherwood was to receive a small commission from the publishing company Finden and Murray as eleven of his illustrations appear in their famous book of 1836, Landscape Illustrations of the Bible, including a view of the Ramesseum, the wonderful "funerary temple" built by Ramses II on the plain of Thebes, and a fine engraving of the Temple of Artemis at Gerasa. A point of interest is that David Roberts also worked on the same book. The

destinations simply by buying a ticket for one of the many "Panoramas" that had sprung up in the big cities. The term "panorama" was originally used to signify the representations of foreign lands that were painted on the inside of huge cylinders; the public entered the cylinders to view the paintings. The sensation of being in a foreign location was heightened by the addition on the ground of bushes, soil, stones, grass and even running water to simulate streams or rivers. This

famous Scottish landscape artist was the author of six volumes of lithographs that were printed between 1842 and 1849 under the title Holy Land, Syria, Idumea, Arabia, Egypt and Nubia. Born in 1796, he was already well-known and working on a collection of lithographs of drawings made during a recent trip through Iberia (published in 1837 with the title Picturesque Sketches in Spain) as well as on the 1836 Landscape Annual published by Jenkins. Anyway, it was Roberts that created the illustration for one of the lithographs that appeared in the two volumes of the Landscape Illustrations of the Bible by refinishing one of the sketches Catherwood made in Jerusalem. The illustration in question is a view of Omar's Mosque. It was quite a common practice at the time for drawings by one artist to be elaborated by another just as it was

there might have existed a relationship between the two artists, however faint.

Anyway, the work for Finden and Murray was not enough to keep Catherwood going, particularly as he had married shortly before. This event is one of the least documented in Frederick's life and it is only from a letter that a friend, James Davies, wrote to Frederick in October 1836 that we hear of the existence of a wife (a young Englishwoman whom he may have met and married in Beirut at the end of 1834 or in London after his return from Palestine). The letter does not mention her name, however. Davies gives the news that he has become a father for the second time and wishes "the same blessing" on Frederick, which suggests that Frederick and his wife were already the parents of one child. In a letter sent by Catherwood to John Bartlett on 25 November 1838 we learn that there is a little boy and that a second

common practice for publishers to copy illustrations for their own books from those of others though, of course, ensuring enough differentiation to prevent accusations of plagiarism. It is a real stroke of misfortune that Roberts, an inveterate letter writer, did not mention this commission. We can only imagine that he had occasion to meet Catherwood and perhaps to view the material that Frederick had brought with him from Egypt and the Holy Land. This possible encounter raises a further hypothesis: that Roberts, whose greatest aspiration was to visit those regions himself one day, was so struck by the pictures shown him that he eventually embarked on the trip that was to bring him everlasting glory in August 1838. It is also fascinating to note that his itinerary retraced nearly all Catherwood's route: perhaps it was simply coincidence and that route was almost obligatory for an artist in search of fame, but it is a pleasing thought that

child has just been born in America but we do not know whether male or female. From a letter sent to Stephens in 1849, we learn that there are now three children and from another letter of the same year that "the boy" is now nearly as tall as Catherwood himself. This would suggest that the first-born was a boy and that he had two sisters. Needless to say, Frederick does not mention the names of either his wife or children in these terse letters and yet nor does Stephens, who had become fairly close to Frederick, actually mention "Mrs Catherwood" by name. We are therefore obliged to fall back on the excerpts of a law suit initiated by Catherwood against the lover of his "wife Gertrude" and assume that the marriage ended in divorce.

What is certain is that, following the "Panorama of Jerusalem", others followed: Athens, Damascus and Algiers plus the ruins of Thebes, Baalbek and Carthage. All were

equally welcomed by the public but, unfortunately, they no longer exist. This may not have been the best way to show the world his talent but it was a method of paying board and lodging, and anyway, fate was about to play another of its tricks. This new work brought him into contact with John Stephens, a young American with red hair and a steady gaze who had travelled far and wide before reaching London. Their meeting was fortunate for both and destined to bring great rewards.

Pages 32, 33 – The Temple of Bacchus at Baalbek by Catherwood in 1834. The same subject appeared in a large "panorama" exhibited in Leicester Square.

Page 33 bottom – This portrait of David Roberts (1796-1864) in oriental dress was made by Robert Lander in 1840. The great Scottish landscape painter is today universally famous for his six volumes of lithographs printed between 1842-49 under the title of "Holy Land, Syria, Idumea, Arabia, Egypt and Nubia".

An unusual lawyer

John Lloyd Stephens can be counted among the handful of 19th century travellers who enjoyed great and long-lasting success. He was born on 28 November 1805 in Shrewsbury, New Jersey, but soon his family moved to New York. It did not seem that art and archaeology were to figure in his life as his parents had planned a brilliant career in law for him, but while he was studying in Illinois (for family reasons) he discovered the attraction that wide open spaces held for him and he was fired with the desire to go down the Mississippi to New Orleans. It was 1824; he succeeded in carrying out his plan but there was no immediate follow-up. He became a lawyer in 1827 but without great enthusiasm and the next year he turned his attentions to political activism on behalf of the Democratic party. He was first involved in the two presidential campaigns of Andew Jackson and in 1834 gave heart and

smelling of home-made bread and spit-roast songbirds. First Stephens went to Italy for its "particularly salubrious climate": after Rome and Naples, he visited Sicily where he began to be interested in archaeological ruins and in particular by the buildings from the Crusader era. In a short time, the lawyer had become a traveller fascinated by antiquities and ruins and ended up following pretty much the same route as Catherwood had done three years earlier. While he was travelling in the newly-independent Greece, Stephens – like Schliemann influenced by Homer and the Iliad – decided to continue eastwards to Turkey.

From April 1835, he started to send letters containing long descriptions of his journeys to his friend Charles Fenno Hoffman, the editor of the American Monthly Magazine. Hoffman started to publish these letters-cum-articles

while he was wandering along the Seine in November, on a bench he found a book by Leon de Laborde published in 1830. It was illustrated with splendid lithographs of a fabulous city excavated from the rock in a hidden wadi in the heart of Arabia Petrea. He immediately postponed all ideas of returning to America and decided to visit Cairo and sail up the Nile. It certainly seems odd that to get to Petra he should

soul to the campaign for the governorship of New York. It was this undertaking that unexpectedly changed his life which was otherwise destined to the "unbearable tedium of the law". He contracted a throat infection from too much public speaking during the campaign and was advised to take a restful trip to Europe by his doctor. It should be remembered that at this time Romanticism was in full flower and travel was considered a panacea for all ills, consequently the Old Continent was filled with the wealthy sick dutifully traipsing around ruined castles, silent monasteries and inns

which became a great success, so launching Stephens on a new career as a journalist. He recorded everything that caught his attention in articulate and brilliant prose, describing the most picturesque sites and reflecting on the events of his unusual experience.

At Constantinople, Stephens embarked for Odessa from where he crossed European Russia to Moscow and St. Petersburg. From there he headed to Warsaw where he was obliged to pass a week while his health improved. Next he stopped at Vienna, then he crossed Germany to reach the long-awaited Paris. Here,

want to travel south through Egypt but once again it turned out to be a stroke of luck. From Alexandria, where he was surprised by the poverty, he was advised to head immediately for Cairo to get a decree issued by the Pasha as the entire region was still not recommended for western travellers. On 1 January 1836, accompanied by his Italian servant Paolo, he headed up the Nile on a comfortable steamer on which he had raised the Stars and Stripes. His diary expresses his excitement at the growing fascination that archaeology held for him: "At Luxor, the colossal skeletons of giant temples are standing

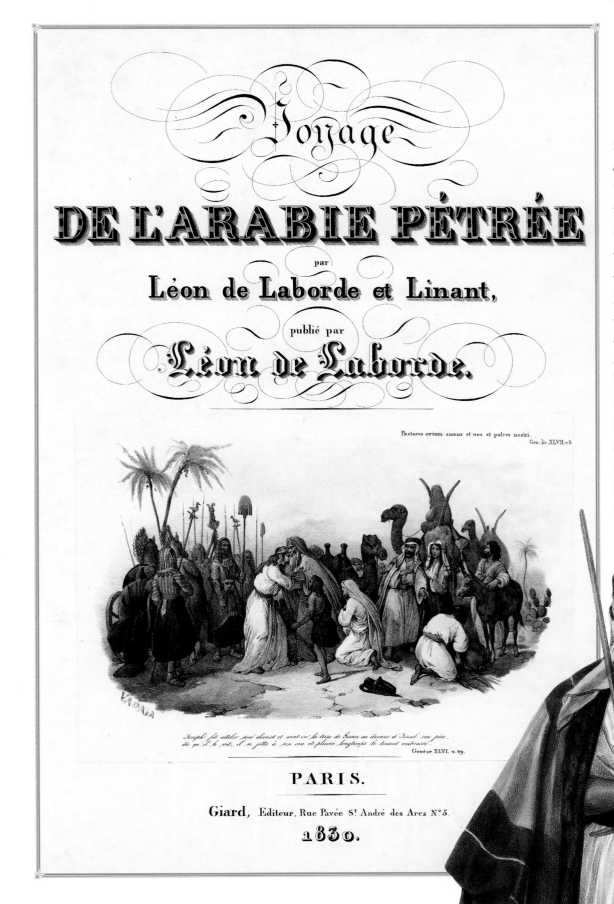

Jongage

DE L'ARABIE PÉTRÉE

par

Léon de Laborde et Linant,

publié par

Léon de Laborde.

Pastores ovium sumus et nos et patres nostri.
Gen: liv. XLVII. v. 3.

Joseph fit atteler son chariot et vint en la terre de Gosen au devant d'Israel son père,
dès qu'il le vit, il se jetta à son cou et pleura longtemps le tenant embrassé.
Genèse XLVI. v. 29.

PARIS.

Giard, Editeur. Rue Pavée St André des Arcs N° 5.

1830.

in the unwatered sands, in solitude and silence". Catherwood had been there less than two years before: once more their paths were crossing. Once back in Cairo, he prepared himself to cross the Sinai in mid-February in the direction of the fabled Petra that the poet John William Burgon had described as the "rose-red city, half as old as time". The desire to see the ancient Nabatean capital in person had been kindled in Stephens by the incredible history of the city carved out of rock; it had been mentioned several times in the Bible with the name of Sela and even then it had been an object of amazement and admiration. On its abandonment, it

Page 34 – This portrait of John Lloyd Stephens (1805-52) was made by Catherwood for the reprint of "Incidents of Travel in Central America, Chiapas and Yucatan" published in London in 1854.

Page 35 top – Frontispiece to "Voyage de l'Arabie Pétrée", the famous work by Léon de Laborde which profoundly influenced John Stephens.

P 35 bottom – Portrait of Léon de Laborde (1807-69) in oriental dress taken from "Voyage de l'Arabie Pétrée", published in Paris in 1830.

fell into oblivion and was only rediscovered in 1812.

While in Cairo, the adventurous lawyer had the good fortune to meet Adolphe Linant de Bellefonds, the famous French explorer, who had made the same journey in 1828 and written an exciting description of his experience. Before leaving, the American decided to improve his chances of safety by buying Arab clothes and a turban in case a disguise might be needed. He then mounted his camel and set off for the unknown. First he stopped at St. Catherine's monastery and climbed Mount Sinai; then he set off across the desert towards Aqaba, suffering from thirst on the way. Finally, he reached his destination in the guise of a Cairo merchant, a common routine for those who wanted to visit Petra and practised by explorers from Burckhardt to David Roberts. The beauty of the ancient town left him speechless. He visited the main monuments – he marvelled at the Khasné, the theatre and the Deir – and then set off again across the desolate Idumea and the hills of Palestine to reach Jerusalem on 12 March. It was here that Stephens learnt the name of Catherwood for the first time when he bought a copy of

Page 36 top – The Khasné, the most famous rock monument in Petra, in a view by Léon de Laborde.

Page 36 bottom – The Deir (or Monastery), another superb example of Nabatean art, illustrated by Léon de Laborde.

the map of the city printed by the English architect the year before. Stephens considered it to be excellent and the finest available. Still not exhausted, he visited Jaffa, the Dead Sea (he was one of the first to realise it was much lower than the level of the Mediterranean), San Saba, Nazareth, Lake Tiberias, Acre, Tyre and Sidon. Then he headed for Beirut. Once he arrived on the coast, he was struck down by a fever and spent ten days in bed but on his recovery he embarked for Alexandria, and then for London.

He reached the city in summer 1836 and soon adapted to the bustle, the throng of traffic, the innumerable goods and the pretty girls in the metropolis. He was soon recognised as the author of the "letters" in the American Monthly and was warmly welcomed by Society as a young and promising star of literature. He did not of course miss the chance to tour the sights, including the Panorama at Leicester Square which was then showing the "View of Jerusalem" painted by Frederick Catherwood. Stephens was greatly impressed and took the opportunity to make his feelings known to the artist. This first meeting was to signal the start of a long-lasting friendship that eventually led to the discovery of the Mayan civilisation, but of course both were ignorant of the momentous events that the future held in store for them. Stephens now wanted nothing more than to return home. Once in New York, he was immediately contacted by the publisher Harper Bros. to offer him a more solid follow-up to his famous "letters".

Stephens therefore found the time to write a detailed account of his adventures called Incidents of Travel in Egypt, Arabia Petrea and the Holy Land, under the unimaginative pseudonym of "An American". His accounts were published in two volumes in 1837 in his customary slightly pedantic but highly effective literary style. The volumes greatly impressed the public and critics – including Edgar Allan Poe – and had enormous commercial success which brought the author the huge sum of 25,000 dollars. The publication was a triumph in all senses: it sold over 20,000 copies in two years, was reprinted for decades and, above all, was the first work by an American author to achieve fame outside the United States.

Page 37 top – The large theatre in Petra, also illustrated by Léon de Laborde.

Page 37 bottom – The famous explorer, geographer and engineer, Adolphe Linant de Bellefonds (1800-83).

CATHERWOOD IN NEW YORK

Catherwood reached New York in 1836. It is generally thought that he decided to go to America on the advice of Stephens, and this is probable, but only after Stephens had left London. Yet some temporal incongruencies in the few documents available make one think that he actually arrived before Stephens who was delayed in London by his worldly commitments. However events took place, in 1836 Catherwood arrived in New York a town which had much to offer someone with the experience and gifts of "Mr Catherwood". It was, for example, a paradise for any architect since Manhattan was a single huge building site in which teams of workers were busy ridding the city of all trace of the disastrous fire in the winter of the previous year. Catherwood – who boasted

membership of the Institute of British Architects and the Royal Architects Society – opened a studio at 94, Greenwich Street with his colleague Frederick Diaper, an English architect in New York who already enjoyed a certain fame. Diaper is today known for his strict classical designs for many buildings on Wall Street, including the Bank of America and the Union Bank, as well as luxurious residences for many of the rich families of the time. Catherwood could easily have followed the example of Diaper but his temperament was different and, above all, his aspiration was to create a "panorama". To this end, once he had established his wife and child in a decorous house on Houston Street, he travelled throughout the state looking for clients while also giving lectures on

his travels in Egypt and the Holy Land. His aim of course was to earn as much money as possible. He spent much of 1837 in this manner and by the end of the year was able to rent a piece of land at Prince Street and Broadway in the centre of Manhattan. Once he had started a company with the bookseller George Jackson, he was finally able to open his own "panorama" in 1838 in which he exhibited his "View of Jerusalem". So while Stephens was drinking from the golden chalice as a result of the success of his book, Catherwood also knew the heady feeling of economic stability. The New Yorkers pushed and shoved to admire the unusual spectacle and the crowds grew bigger every day. Part of its success was due to the publicity his friend Stephens had given it,

Page 38 bottom – A view of New York in the first half of the 19th century after reconstruction following the great fire in 1835.

Pages 38, 39 – Brooklyn (left) and Manhattan (right) can be recognised in this pre-1850 view of New York.

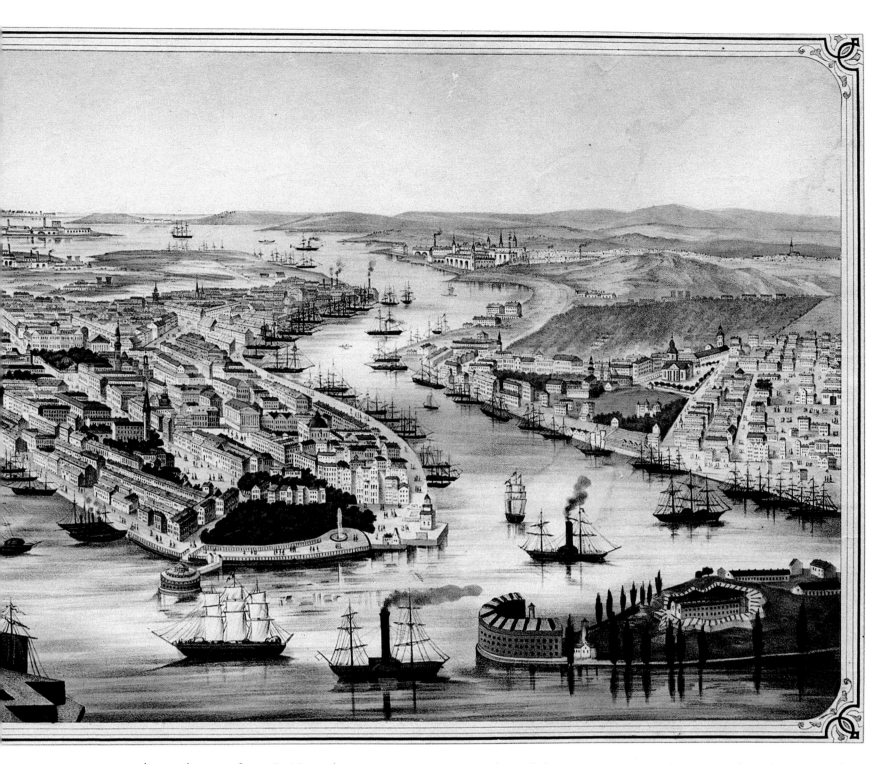

exploiting his own fame. In November 1838, a father for the second time, Frederick made a quick trip to London to bring the gigantic canvases made years before for Robert Burford to New York. The "Panorama of Catherwood and Jackson" was by now a profitable and well-established business. This was the first entertainment of this kind in the United States and was to be visited by thousands of people in the years to come. The canvases were on average nearly 3000 square feet in size, they were lit by more than 200 gas lamps and the entrance ticket cost only 25 cents. It is understandable why the

main newspapers welcomed the attraction so enthusiastically and now New York too had its window on the world thanks to the "notable talent and brilliant artistry of Mr Catherwood". The panorama of Thebes was particularly well received and Frederick considered temporarily transferring his colossal views (to which he had added another of the Niagara Falls) to the main cities on the east coast: Boston, Philadelphia and Providence.

In the meantime, Stephens had been contacted by John Russell Bartlett who had established a publishing company with Charles Welford in

1837. It was Bartlett who suggested a trip to Central America to discover the mysterious cities lost in the jungle which had been spoken of in cultural circles for so long. To stimulate his curiosity further, Bartlett sent Stephens a selection of books with enigmatic illustrations showing temples and other strange buildings of uncommon architectural styles. Curious by nature and fascinated by the monuments of the Yucatán, still an almost unknown corner of the world, Stephens studied the books and then applied himself to research in archives and libraries. What he learnt radically altered the course of his life and that of "Mr Catherwood".

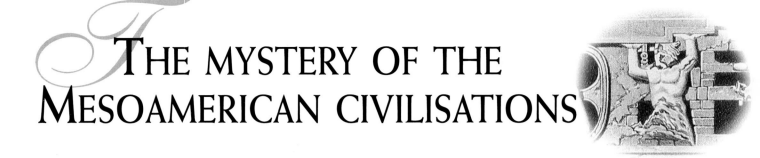
At the beginning of the 19th century, the native inhabitants of the New World were little more than savages to the Americans of European origin. They were people that devoted themselves to unnameable rites, barbarians devoid of any ethical or technical knowledge and incapable of creating the remotest semblance of civilisation. People like George Catlin, Karl Bodmer and Charles Bird King, who had lived among the Indians of North America and proclaimed them noble of spirit and soul, were looked upon with suspicion if not with open hostility. Even the peoples that had populated Central America before the arrival of the Conquistadors did not

the Egyptians, the Phoenicians, the Vikings and even the Chinese. Even the adventurers that had entered the jungles and seen the superb ruins of temples and palaces with their own eyes could not admit that they were the work of indigenous peoples. In his book Teatro Critico Americano published in 1822, Doctor Pablo Felix Cabrera supported the thesis that the Central American ruins had an Egyptian origin. The most common theory, however mad it seems today, was that Central America had been

Page 40 – The Palace at Palenque in a drawing by Luciano Castañeda.

Pages 40, 41 – In this reproduction of a glyphic inscription found at Palenque, Waldeck did not hesitate to insert non-existent elements like the elephant's head visible in the second row from the top, on the right.

merit more attention and the accounts written by Hernán Cortés, Bernal Díaz del Castillo and other missionaries, leaders and their 16th century contemporaries were either unknown or considered works of unbridled imagination. Those few who believed in the existence of these mysterious peoples either thought they were uncivilised and bloodthirsty or that they had arrived in America from Europe, Africa or Asia. There were those who believed them descendants of

colonized in some ancient time by the "lost tribes of Israel" and many scholars were ready to recognise without any doubt that the physiognomies of the Indians had "evident Semitic features". The Austrian count, Jéan-Frédéric Waldeck, was one of the first Europeans to visit Palenque and he claimed that it was the Chaldeans that founded the city while the rest of the population of the Yucatán was of Hindu origin. To support his jumbled

hypothesis, he even included symbols in an Egyptian style and cuneiform signs in the drawings he made among the ruins of the lost city, all of which were imaginary. In his book Voyage pittoresque et Archaeologique dans la Province de Yucatán, published in Paris in 1838, however wonderful a proof it is of an outstanding artistic talent, it remains an eloquent example of the mystification that was practised in those years. Even the technically reliable drawings of

Page 41 – Count Jean Fréderic Waldeck (1766-1875) was an able artist but also an unscrupulous deceiver. In these two tables showing stucco panels at Palenque, the clothes and head-dresses (one has even been shown similar to an elephant) have been distorted to seem more classical in style.

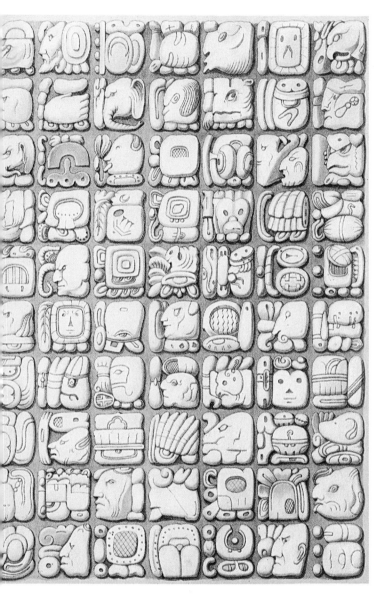

Mexican artist Luciano Castañeda, who accompanied Captain Guillelmo Dupaix from 1805-07 in exploration of the ruins of Palenque and other sites, are a perfect example of how he and his colleagues did not understand what they were reproducing and that they were utterly incapable of faithfully bearing witness to a style they had never seen before.

Similarly, the missionaries, army officers, functionaries and adventurers that had written about the temples and objects buried in the forests in their accounts were not able to free themselves from their ethnocentrism and lack of imagination that rendered them irremediably blind to the evidence. No-one wanted to pay attention to names like Aztec, Mixtec, Toltec and Maya that had been passed down from the Conquistadors as being distinct peoples: the thinking was that all Indians were the descendants of the Jews that had come to the new world after the Flood. Few dared to put this sacrosanct "truth" in doubt. One of them was a colonel of the Guatemalan army that had published a book in 1835 called Descricción de las ruinas de Copán *that contained many drawings of the site and its buildings where he had carried out a rudimentary exploration and excavation the year before. Juan Galindo, too, must have had great intuition as he was the first to identify the hieroglyphic writing that he had seen at Copán and Palenque as being exclusive to the Mayan culture. It was Galindo's work, published in Paris in 1834 with the title* Antiquités Mexicaines, *that above all attracted the attention of Stephens and kindled his enthusiasm. Unlike his contemporaries, the lawyer was under the impression that at some remote time in the past, a magnificent civilisation had flourished in Central America, the art and archaeology of which needed to be studied on the spot. There was no lack of money as the income from his book* Incidents of Travel in Arabia Petrea, *in addition to that to come from* Incidents of Travel in Greece, Turkey, Russia and Poland, *published in 1838 by Harper Bros.,* were more than enough to finance an expedition. Three names were fixed in his mind, they were Copán, Palenque and Uxmal. These were the cities he was to search for in the jungles of Central America. Stephens was not the first to tread this path: in 1832, a French doctor named Corroy had written on one of the walls of the "Palace" at Palenque that he had been there three times — and accompanied by his wife and children — but he was certainly the first to try to interpret its secrets with objectivity.

Once roused, Stephens was not a man to give in to obstacles. He began preparations and alerted Catherwood to his plans. Catherwood naturally volunteered to go with him without hesitation, which was exactly what the American needed: a trusted and experienced companion, unwavering when confronted by difficulties and, above all, an excellent artist. In a world where photography still did not exist (the Frenchman Louis-Jacques Daguerre had developed his first photographic plate in 1837 but it would be some years before pictures could be printed), artists played a fundamental role in scientific expeditions. It was they who provided

proof of and spread news of discoveries. Catherwood, who had spent much of his youth travelling in Egypt and Palestine, was fascinated by the descriptions of Palenque, the lost city in the jungle of Chiapas. Frederick had studied in depth the greatest architectural ruins around the Mediterranean and down the White Nile and he was sceptical of the theories that were currently in vogue. The buildings, sculptures and bas-reliefs that Stephens had shown him in the books sent him by Bartlett did not seem to have anything to do with the art of the Old World and, in particular, the drawings made by Waldeck seemed similarly suspect.

As the two firmed up their plans, chance lent a hand once more. In September 1839, the newly elected American chargé d'affaires in the Central American Federation suddenly died leaving the post vacant. Stephens, who had always been a Democrat, asked the Democrat President Van Buren if he could have the post. The New York lawyer was a well-known figure, though for his literary success rather than his political militancy, and had the backing of several influential people. However he got what he wanted and on 13 August he received an official letter which asked him to leave as soon as possible. His instructions were not clear, especially as the political situation in Central America was rather confused, but for Stephens this was a secondary detail. His position guaranteed him diplomatic immunity and that was what he needed. Once he had arrived at his destination, he could discharge his political duties as quickly as possible and then dedicate himself to searching for the lost cities of the Maya. In order to give himself an appearance fitting to his role, he had a blue uniform made up fitted with plenty of gold buttons. It was a gaudy dress uniform that, in its way, was to be extremely useful. On 9 September, Stephens and Catherwood – who had handed over management of the Panorama to his partner, Jackson – signed an agreement in which the first agreed to pay all the

travel expenses and to guarantee payment of 1,500 dollars for the exclusive rights to use the graphical material produced on the trip.

Catherwood agreed not to publish either drawings or accounts of his journey until Stephens gave his permission. After receiving 200 dollars on account, Frederick signed. Everything was ready, their greatest adventure was about to begin.

Pages 42, 43 – Waldeck has sneakily altered the shape of the mountain in this view of Palenque to make it look like a pyramid.

Page 43 – This is the last page of the contract signed between Stephens and Catherwood on 9 September 1839.

Page 42 – The drawing shows a bas-relief at Palenque. The Phrygian cap of the person on the throne, the cuneiform symbols and the Pan's pipe in the column of glyphs on the left are all the result of Waldeck's imagination.

THE MAYA REDISCOVERED

At this point of our story, a short digression about who the Maya were and the type of civilisation they created is appropriate. Questions regarding their civilisation are greatly answered by study of Catherwood's magnificent illustrations, published in 1844 after his two adventurous trips of exploration through the forests of Central America and across the plains of the Yucatán. For that reason, the tables which originally appeared with the title Views of Ancient Monuments in Central America, Chiapas and Yucatan, even then considered his masterpiece, are published here.

The twenty-six hand-coloured lithographs with his own descriptions are more illuminating and explicit than many learned discourses. Surprisingly detailed, they show without doubt that the Maya were the authors of some of the most artistic and intellectual works

of pre-Columbian America. Besides large constructions, the Maya produced works of artistic refinement such as stone and plaster sculptures, frescoes, painted pottery and bas-reliefs in wood.

Developing out of the fertile culture created by the Olmecs (the people that spread across the Mexican highlands and along the Pacific coast as far as Guatemala during the 1st millennium BC), the Mayan civilisation reached its peak during the Classical Period between 250 – 950 AD. They controlled a huge area which covered what are today Guatemala and Belize and part of Honduras and El Salvador plus the Mexican regions of Chiapas and Tabasco. The Maya created centralised states guided by hereditary rulers often in conflict with each other. A flourishing economy based on intensive agriculture and trade of

valuable goods such as jade, cocoa beans, obsidian, feathers and cotton encouraged rapid growth in the number of urban centres connected by an efficient road network. Their social organisation grew complex: at its head was the ruler who held political and military power and was responsible for the well-being of the community on a spiritual level. Society was rigidly divided by a hierarchy with priests and nobles at the top, then warriors, merchants, craftsmen, farmers and, at the bottom, slaves. Cities, some of which – such as Tikal, Copán, Palenque, Piedras Negras, El Mirador and many others – grew until they had populations of tens of thousands, they were built around monumental ceremonial centres, markets and large public buildings used for administration. Temples and palaces were built from stone; they were often plastered and

Page 45 – The frontespiece of Views of Ancient Monuments is by Owen Jones (1804-74), an architect and draughtsman who was actively interested in decorative problems.

VIEWS

OF

ANCIENT MONVMENTS

IN

CENTRAL AMERICA

CHIAPAS

AND

YVCATAN

BY

F. CATHERWOOD, ARCH.

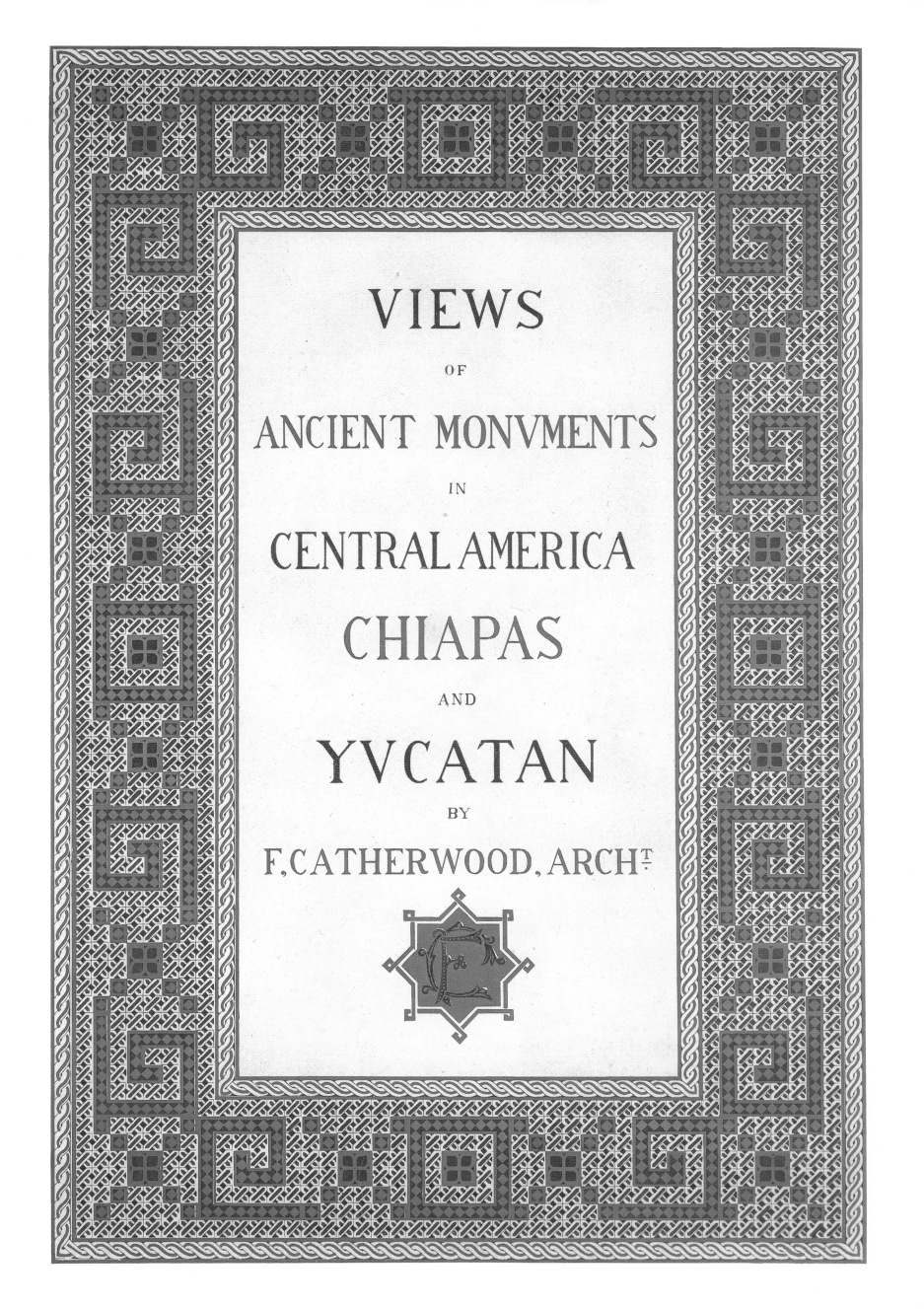

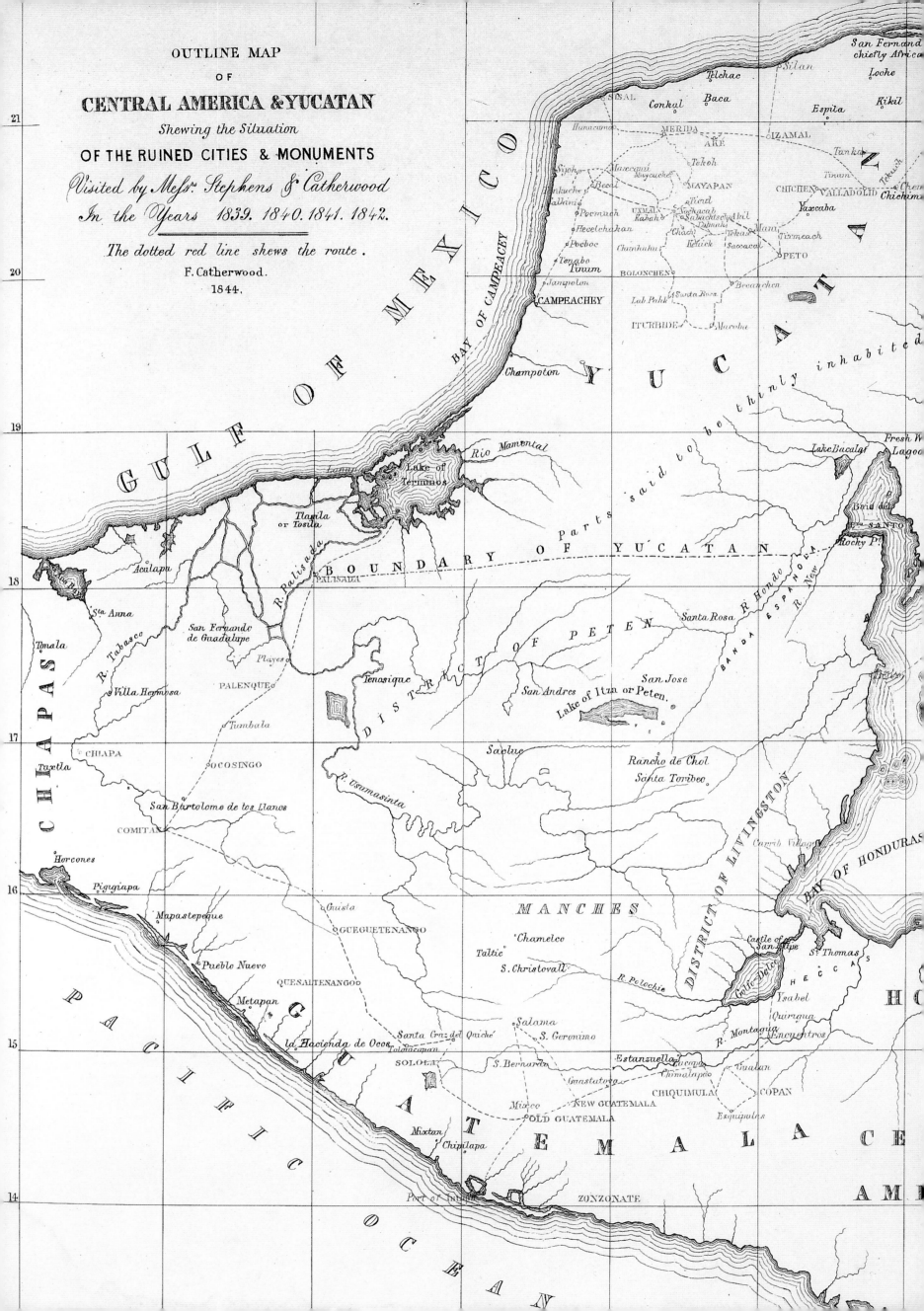

OUTLINE MAP

OF

CENTRAL AMERICA & YUCATAN

Shewing the Situation

OF THE RUINED CITIES & MONUMENTS

Visited by Messrs. Stephens & Catherwood

In the Years 1839. 1840. 1841. 1842.

The dotted red line shews the route.

F. Catherwood.

1844.

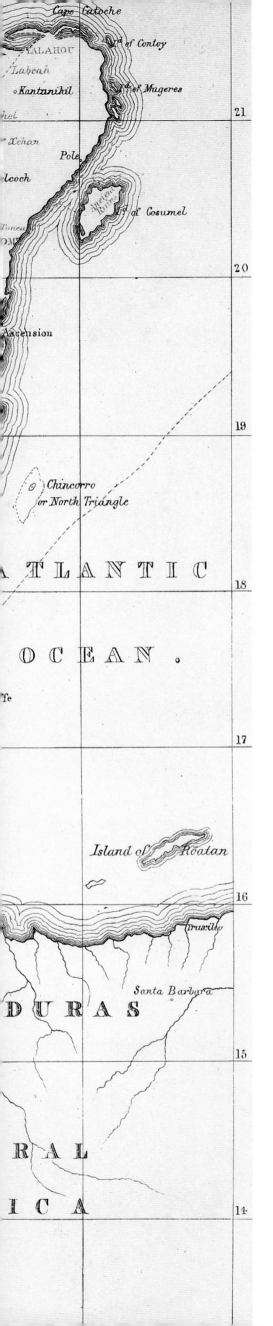

painted red or white and decorated with bas-reliefs, stuccoes and frescoes. Residential buildings were made from wood and plaster and had straw roofs.

The Maya never built a true arch but they used a false vault in its place. Nor did they use the wheel, above all because they did not have the animals which would have made the use of carts possible: oxen and horses were only introduced after the Spanish conquest.

The Maya also developed the most complex form of writing in pre-Columbian America and their extremely advanced knowledge of mathematics made possible their amazing understanding of astronomy and the calendar.

Despite their basic cultural uniformity, the most important cities developed their own architectural and figurative styles, mirroring their autonomy in political affairs and their independent military and economic control of surrounding regions. Naturally, accounts of the conflicts between the cities are reported in detail in the decorations of the main city buildings with the names of the victorious and defeated kings. Exhaustive examples are the stelae at Copán and Quiriguá, the polychrome stucco panels found at Palenque and the frescoes at Bonampak. The period of maximum splendour of the Mayan civilisation at the end of the 10th century was followed by a rapid and still mysterious decline. Perhaps it was caused by an epidemic or by famine due to over-exploitation of the land or by climatic changes following deforestation. The result was that all the main Mayan cities in the central highlands were abandoned within a hundred years. At almost the same time, new important Maya cities were built in the Yucatán and a second phase of grandeur was experienced. At Uxmal, Chichén Itzá, Sayil, Kabah and many other smaller cities, the architecture and applied arts reached an extraordinary level of refinement in

the extremely elaborate Puuc style but this phase of cultural rebirth was short-lived as the Yucatán peninsula was invaded during the 10th century by the Toltecs, a people from central Mexico. The Toltecs were strongly militarised and introduced the cult of the Plumed Serpent (Kukulcán), mass human sacrifices and less elaborate artistic forms. The latter can be best admired in the Castillo, the Pyramid of the Warriors, the huge ball-court and other monuments at Chichén Itzá.

It was Chichén Itzá that played the dominant role around 1200 AD but this city was soon ousted by Mayapán. Then, at the end of the 16th century, the Mayan-Toltec political unity was split definitively into a large number of city-states such as Tulum.

The Maya that still lived in the southern regions were subjugated by the Spanish in 1526 while those who fled to the wilderness of Petén held out until 1697. Today about 2.5 million Maya survive, divided into 28 different linguistic groups.

The tables that follow are described by Catherwood's original comments in italics. Any other notes that have been considered necessary are in normal type. Note that the 19th-century place-names have been maintained as has improper use of the term teocalli (temples) which actually belongs to the Aztec language, Nahuatl.

To conclude, let it be remembered that, in an age when the most bizarre theories on the origin of the Maya were widespread — that they were descended from the Egyptians, the Jews or some other even more improbable stock — Catherwood was a unique case: studying only the objective data, he tried to see and reproduce what was before him with a soul free from prejudice. Indeed he succeeded and it is in his formidable objectivity that his greatness lies.

Pages 46-47 – The Map of Central America contained in Frederick Catherwood's work.

PLATE I

*I*DOL, AT COPÁN

The Plate gives a front view of one of the most perfect of a group of eleven. They were all deeply buried amidst tropical trees when first discovered, and it was with no small difficulty that a sufficient space was cleared away to admit of a drawing being made. The Idol is carved out of a single block of compact limestone, and measures eleven feet eight inches in height, and three feet four inches on each side, standing on a pedestal six feet square. It is surrounded by a circular stone curb or rim, measuring, in its outer diameter, sixteen feet six inches. A sacrificial stone, or altar, stands in front of it, at a distance of eight feet ten inches, but is not introduced into the drawing, as it would have hidden the lower part of the figure. It is placed diagonally towards the Idol, measuring seven feet across. There is every probability (from the deep groovings, or channels, on all the altars) that they were used for the immolation of human victims. The Idol, viewed in front, represents a woman of middle age, with the arms curiously raised and bent before her; the wrists are adorned with bracelets of beads, and the neck profusely covered with necklaces; on either side of the head descends a tress of hair; the ears are large, unnatural in their shape, and are decorated with ear-drops; immediately over the forehead appears a row of beads attached to the hair. The head-dress is not easy to describe: it is very lofty, and one of its peculiarities is a skull, or upper part of the head of some animal, the lower jaw being wanting. Whether the remainder of the head-dress is intended to represent feathers, or flowers, or a mixture of the two, is doubtful. The lower part of the dress has the appearance of a cotton robe (cotton being indigenous to the country, and much used), ornamented with chequer work, and fringed with beads. The feet are clothed in sandals of precisely the same form as are found in some of the old Roman statues; they appear to have been a conspicuous part of the dress. The sides of the Idol have rows of hieroglyphics, and the back is as elaborately carved as the front, but the subject is totally different. It presents a mask, surrounded by complicated ornaments, with a gracefully disposed border, and, at the base, rows of hieroglyphics.

Copán, the vast archeological site located in present-day Honduras, is famous for the fifty or so stelae spread around the monumental centre. The stelae are peculiar to the Mayan civilisation and generally depict an upright king assimilated by the rising sun while he escapes from the jaws of the terrestrial monster whose figure occupies the space behind. Usually stelae are inscribed with dates, historical facts, astronomical information and religious text. Raised in 730 AD, Stele H is the only one at Copán that shows a female figure (although the possibility exists that it is really a king dressed in women's clothing) though the reason why this should be is not known. The figure, standing in an unnatural posture, holds the symbol of power, the two-headed snake sceptre, in her hands.

PLATE II

PYRAMIDAL BUILDING AND FRAGMENTS OF SCULPTURE, AT COPÁN

This drawing represents one of the most remarkable and perfect monuments at Copan. It is a pyramidal structure, or perhaps, more correctly speaking, part of an immense terraced mound. The top, being broad and level, was probably used as a foundation for small temples, or for statues, though no traces of the former remain; and of the latter, the fragments are so much shattered, that it is impossible to ascertain where they originally stood. The height of the pyramidal terrace is about thirty-five feet; it is composed of small stones, well laid in mortar, and when in a perfect state was encrusted with a coating of stucco. Several fragments of sculptured ornament have been introduced into the foreground of this Plate, though found at some distance from the building. The colossal skull of a monkey is seen in the left-

hand corner: it was, perhaps, an object of worship. The monkey tribe inhabit the forests of Copan in great numbers, and may frequently be seen watching attentively the movements of the traveller, or leaping from branch to branch on the tops of the high trees, causing a noise like the rushing of a fierce wind. In the foreground is a round altar, or sacrificial stone, with the grooves visible, by which, probably, the blood of the victim ran to the ground. Standing against the tree is the bust of a warrior, or cacique; and next to it, the portrait of some distinguished chieftain. The head-dress is unfortunately broken. To the right of the picture are the feet and sandals of a statue, which, in point of design and workmanship, would not have disgraced a Roman artist of the olden time.

⌐╦╦╦╦╦╦╦╦╦╦╦╦╦╦⌐

In all probability, the drawing shows the acropolis seen from the extreme south of the Great Square. It is easier to recognise part of Stele 4 in the sculptural details and the roundish shape of its altar.

⌐╦╦╦╦╦╦╦╦╦╦╦╦╦╦⌐

PLATE III

BACK OF AN IDOL, AT COPÁN

The subject of this Plate is the back
of one of the stone Idols at Copan. The
design consists of five wreaths,
enclosing hieroglyphics. They are
sculptured with the greatest care, and
traces of red paint are in some places
just discernible. The outer border
appears intended to represent leaves tied
together with ribbon, forming bows.
The whole composition is at once
chaste and elegant, and very unlike the
generality of the sculpture at Copan,
which would seem rather intended to
inspire fear and horror than any
gentler emotion ; this, on the contrary,
is so graceful and pleasing, that instead
of human sacrifices, it may well be
supposed that nothing but fruits and
flowers were offered before it. The
entanglement of a tropical forest is
given in the back-ground.

Stelae are independent monolith
monuments sculpted from a single rock
and generally carved on all four sides.
They were part of the development of the
Maya civilisation for roughly six centuries.
The oldest known is Stele 29 at Tikal
which has been dated to 292 AD while
the most recent is Stele 102 at Toniná,
dating from 909. Stele F at Copán, which
Catherwood drew from behind, was
raised in 721.

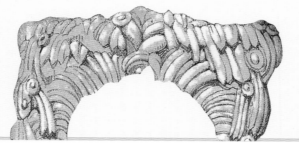

PLATE IV

Broken idol, at Copán

This Idol, in its ruined state, is one of the most beautiful in Copan ; and in workmanship, is equal to the best remains of Egyptian art. Its present condition may give some idea of the scene of desolation and ruin presented at Copan. The whole region is an overgrown forest; and, amidst the prostration and wreck of buildings and terraces, one "Idol" is seen displaced from its pedestal by monstrous roots,æanother locked in the close embrace of branches of trees, and almost lifted out of the earth, and another hurled to the ground, and bound down by large vines and creepers: of this, the fallen part was thus completely bound to the earth, and, before it could be drawn, it was necessary to unlace them, and tear the fibres out of the crevices. The fallen statue is of about the same dimensions with the others. The paint is very perfect, and has preserved the stone, which makes it more to be regretted that it is broken. The altar is buried, with the top barely visible, which, by excavating, we made out to represent the back of a tortoise.

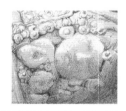

Today completely restored, Stele C stands in Copán's central square. It is carved from a single block of andesite 13 feet high and is dated to 782. It shows the Rising Sun, sixteenth and last ruler of the superb Maya city, who ascended the throne in 763 and died in 800. During his long reign, the acropolis was completely rebuilt and the city lived through a period of unequalled splendour.

PLATE V

Idol and altar, at Copán

In this Plate, the altar, or sacrificial stone, forms the principal object in the fore-ground. It is three feet six inches high, above the ground, and measures seven feet from angle to angle. It is sculptured into four hideous heads of colossal size, having enormous fangs, and distended eyes, adding, no doubt, the finishing horror to the bloody sacrifices which there can be little doubt were enacted on it. Certain channels (now nearly obliterated) exist on its upper surface, to carry off the blood of the human victim ; and to render the operation of cutting open the breast, and tearing out the heart more easy, the upper surface of the stone is slightly convex, agreeing with the accounts of the early Spanish discoverers. It was painted red, a fitting colour for so sanguinary a ritual. The Idol, to whom the sacrifice was offered, stands at a distance of twelve feet from the sacrificial stone. It is eleven feet nine inches high, and three feet square, cut out of a single block of stone, and has elaborate carvings on the back and sides. It is conjectured to be the portrait of some deified hero or chieftain, from certain traces of individuality in the features. There are remains of a beard and moustache, and the whole figure is enveloped and overladen with a complicated dress and head ornaments. It stands at the foot of a pyramidal terrace, or wall, which probably supported the sacred edifice.

The table shows what is now known as Stele D and its extraordinary altar which perhaps shows the god of death, Ah Puch. This monolith stands at the northern end of the Great Square, in front of the steps that lead to Temple 2. It is dated to 736 and is one of Copán's oldest altars.

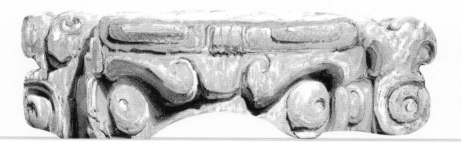

PLATE VI

GENERAL VIEW OF PALENQUE

The ruins of Palenque are the first which awakened the attention to the existence of ancient and unknown cities in America.

They lie twelve miles distant, in a south-easterly direction from Palenque, the last village northward in the State of Chiapas. They have no other name than that of the village near which they are situated, but in the neighbourhood they are called "Las Casas de Piedra," or, "the Houses of Stone."

The extent of the ruin is not very great, at least, so far as we were able to survey; and we visited all the buildings mentioned by Del Rio and Dupaix. A square space, one thousand yards each way, would include them all; but the extent of ground is apparently much larger, which deception, no doubt, arises from the difficulty and time required to pass from one spot to another, from the extreme denseness of the tropical vegetation.

The largest and most important

structure is called the Palace, seen to the left in the drawing. The principal front faces the east, and is the opposite one to that shown by the drawing. It measures two hundred and twenty-eight feet, and the same on the rear. The two side-fronts each measure one hundred and eighty feet. Its height does not exceed twenty-five feet, and all around it had a bold projecting cornice of stone. It stands on an artificial mound, forty feet high, three hundred and ten feet front and rear, and two hundred and sixty feet on each side. These are its principal dimensions. The front and rear had each fourteen doorways, and the ends, eleven. The openings are about nine feet wide, and the piers between six and seven feet. The entire building was of stone, stuccoed and painted, with spirited bas reliefs on the piers, and projecting borders of hieroglyphics, and other ornaments. It had three principal court-yards, the largest of which is given in the following Plate. There are several

interesting portions of stone sculpture, and of paintings in colours, connected with this building; the latter, especially, is being fast obliterated by the excessive dampness prevailing the greater part of the year. The vegetation, at the time of our visit, was close and rank, and it was not without considerable labour, in the cutting away of trees, that the entire design of the building could be made out.

In the fore-ground of the drawing is seen an elevated pyramidal mound, which appears once to have had steps on all its sides. These steps have been thrown down by the growth of trees, making the ascent very difficult. The mound, measured on the slope, is one hundred and ten feet. On the platform, at top, is a stone Casa, or House, seventy-six feet in front, and twenty-five feet deep. It has doors and piers still standing, the end piers being ornamented with hieroglyphics, and the centre ones with figures. The interior of the building

is divided into two corridors, running lengthways, with ceilings formed of over-lapping stones, rising nearly to a point, and floors paved with large square stones. The corridors are each seven feet wide, separated by a massive wall, and the back one divided into three chambers. The centre room contains a stone tablet of hieroglyphics, and there are two others in the front corridor. The roof is inclined, and the sides are covered with stucco ornaments, now much broken, but enough remains to show that it must, when perfect, have been rich and imposing. On the top was a range of small square piers, covered by a layer of flat projecting stones, which gives it the appearance of a low open balustrade.

The two Casas in the distance, and to the right of the high mound, are very similar in construction to the one just described. They were richly ornamented both with sculpture and painting, as also with works in stucco. Each stands on its respective mound, with stone staircases, now overgrown with trees and shrubs. There are two other Casas of smaller dimensions, but so much ruined that little more than their outline remains.

The high hill, in the back-ground of the picture, appeared so regular that, but for its great height (nearly one thousand feet), we should have supposed it artificial. On the summit are the remains of an ancient structure.

It is due to the reader to state, that this general view of Palenque is composed of separate sketches of each Casa, or Building, and from the ground-plan each is made to occupy its respective position. No other method could be adopted, as the large size of the trees, and dense nature of the forest, precluded any idea of making a clearing sufficient to embrace them all in one view. The clearing is, therefore, not real, but imaginary. The remainder of the drawing may be considered as quite faithful..

Palenque was in fact much larger than Catherwood thought. The site stretches on three different levels for a little over 2 miles from east to west and for more than half a mile north to south. Only a small part has so far been systematically explored and restored. The "pyramidal tumulus" described by Catherwood is today known as the Pyramid of the Inscriptions due to the hieroglyphic texts inside the temple on the top of the structure. The "balustrade" is all that remains of the tall perforated crest that crowned the temple and that was typical of sacred Mayan buildings in Chiapas and Campeche. It should also be noted, despite what the author says, that the illustration is not exact as the mountain is actually directly behind the pyramid: this is an example of Romantic "poetic licence" which Catherwood took to make the view more attractive.

PLATE VII

PRINCIPAL COURT OF THE PALACE AT PALENQUE

In the preceding Plate, a distant view of the Palace at Palenque is given. The present drawing represents a portion of the principal court-yard, which is eighty feet long, and seventy wide, and surrounded on the four sides with open corridors. A portion of this corridor is given in the Plate; each opening is nine feet wide, and the piers six feet. These latter are of stone, covered with stucco, and ornamented with figures, painted. The lintels were of wood, and have in all cases fallen. The superincumbent masonry was covered with stuccoed ornaments, now nearly obliterated. We found large trees growing on the roofs. A flight of stone steps, thirty feet broad, lead down into the court-yard (see Plate). On either side of the steps are grim and gigantic figures, carved on stone, in basso relievo, nine feet high, inclined back towards the corridor at the same angle as the steps. The attitudes of the figures are constrained and awkward, but not altogether destitute of expression. Two of the figures have hieroglyphics carved on what appear to be aprons suspended from their waists, and all have ornamented head-dresses, with necklaces, ear-rings, &c.

The table shows a part of the north-east court and Building A inside the Palace. The bas-reliefs described by Catherwood depict figures in an act of submission to the ruler of Palenque: they are clearly important people (as shown by their jewellery) but their status as prisoners is represented by the absence of belts and head-dresses.

PLATE VII BIS

Interior of House No III., Palenque

This Interior is given with a view of showing the peculiar triangular arch of the country, formed of stones, each projecting beyond the other, until at last they nearly meet at top, and are covered by a flat stone. The ancient manner of hanging doors is also seen. Semicircular holes were cut in the door jambs, holding small round stones, on which, by a simple contrivance, the doors might be made to turn. The building measures, on the outside, thirty-eight feet by twenty-eight, and stands on a lofty mound. It has three doorways leading to a corridor, thirty-two feet long by nine feet wide, which communicates with three rooms; the centre one measures eighteen feet by nine feet, and contains some interesting bas reliefs, beautifully cut in stone. The whole exterior of the front was richly ornamented with painted stuccoes.

What Catherwood called House 3 is today known as the Temple of the Foliated Cross, named after an unusual stucco decoration which actually is a representation of the "Sacred Tree". Incontrovertible proof has not yet found that confirms Catherwood's opinion on the existence of doors inside Mayan constructions. A theory has been put forward that the cavities noted by the Englishman were simply used to hang cord from one post to another to support heavy drapes. The debate is still open. It is possible to see in the foreground what seems to be a round arch; in fact, this singular configuration is completely accidental and was probably due to the collapse of a wooden architrave and a portion of the wall above.

PLATE VIII

GENERAL VIEW OF LAS MONJAS, AT UXMAL

This view is taken from the upper terrace of the Governor's House (Casa del Gobernador), looking northwards. It embraces the whole of the buildings called "Las Monjas" (or the "Nuns"), forming the centre distance of the drawing. This building is quadrangular, with a court-yard in the centre, two hundred and fourteen feet wide, and two hundred and fifty-eight feet deep. The centre building, and the most distant, is two hundred and sixty-four feet long, standing on a terrace twenty feet high; and above the cornice, from one end to the other, it was ornamented with sculpture. (For a specimen, see Plate XV.) The ascent to the terrace is by a grand, but ruined staircase, ninety-five feet wide, having ruined buildings on either side. The height to the second cornice is twenty-five feet, and the highest portions were forty-two feet. The stone carving was most elaborate. There are several statues remaining on this front, representing players on musical instruments. The instruments resemble the modern harp and guitar. The back front was also elaborately ornamented, and several of the figures and the decorations still remain. This building encloses one of older date; the doorways, walls, and wooden lintels of the latter are all seen, and a richly ornamented cornice is visible where the outer building is destroyed. The front had fourteen outer doorways, and

fourteen inner doorways, leading to twenty-eight rooms, all of which are covered with the triangular arch. The building which forms the right, or eastern side of the quadrangle, is one hundred and fifty-eight feet long, with five doorways and fourteen rooms, richly decorated on the exterior and ends. The edifice on the left, or western side, is one hundred and seventy-three feet long, with seven doorways and fourteen rooms. On the facade are the remains of a colossal serpent. (See Plate XIV.) This interesting subject is, unfortunately, in a most dilapidated state, and the little that remains is in such a tottering condition, that a few more rainy seasons will probably prostrate the whole. The front centre building is two hundred and seventy-nine feet long, having twenty doorways and as many rooms. In the centre is an arched doorway, ten feet eight inches wide, which leads into the great court-yard, and was apparently the only entrance to it. The facades of this building are not so richly ornamented with sculpture as either of the others; but they possess a chasteness and simplicity which give them a peculiar interest.

On the right of the drawing is seen the great Teocallis, or the Diviner's House, surmounted by a building described at Plate XII.; and just beneath it, westward, is the gateway described in Plate XI. There were staircases both on the east and west sides of this Teocallis.

Uxmal was founded in the 10th century; it is one of the principal Mayan sites in the whole of Yucatán. Of the various monuments in the cultural centre, the Nunnery Quadrangle is the most impressive. The facades of the different sides of the buildings are covered with stone mosaic tiles in geometric patterns which alternate with large masks of the god Chac with the prominent nose. Together

they give the architectural design a surprising and rare elegance. The bas-reliefs showing the two-headed celestial snake and the Plumed Serpent, repeated hundreds of times, are reminiscent of Mayan religious themes but also of the Mexican religious world which was brought to Uxmal by Toltec invaders. The scale reproductions of some of the huts are fundamental documentary evidence of the appearance of Mayan houses.

PLATE IX

ORNAMENT OVER THE PRINCIPAL DOORWAY, CASA DEL GOBERNADOR, AT UXMAL

The "Casa del Gobernador," or House of the Governor, is one of the most extensive and important of the ancient buildings at Uxmal, in Yucatan. It is constructed entirely of hewn stone, and measures three hundred and twenty feet in front, by forty feet in depth. The height is about twenty-six feet. It has eleven doorways in front, and one at each end. The apartments are narrow, seldom exceeding twelve feet, just large enough to swing a hammock, which was, and still is, the substitute for beds throughout the country. Some of the rooms measure sixty feet in length, and are twenty-three feet high. There does not appear to have been any internal decoration in the chambers, nor are there any windows. The lower part of the edifice is of plain wrought stone, but the upper portion is singularly rich in ornament, a fragment of it is shown in the drawing. Taking the front, the ends, and the rear of the building, there is a length of seven hundred and fifty-two feet of elaborate carving, on which traces of colour are still visible. The peculiar arch of the country has been employed in every room. The lintels of

the doorways were of wood, a more costly material to work than stone, but less durable. Unfortunately they have all decayed, and the masonry they supported has, in places, fallen down (see Plate), and much of the beauty of the building is thus destroyed. The central ornament over the principal doorway was a seated figure, of which but slight traces remain. The head-dress of feathers is more perfect, and appears totally disproportioned to the size of the figure. On either side are parallel bars of stone, between which are well sculptured hieroglyphics. The cornice was perhaps intended to represent the coilings of a serpent; it is continued from one extremity of the building to the other, and goes entirely round it. The Casa del Gobernador stands on three terraces, the lowest is three feet high, fifteen feet wide, and five hundred and seventy-five feet long; the second is twenty feet high, two hundred and fifty feet wide, and five hundred and forty-five feet long; and the third is nineteen feet high, thirty feet broad, and three hundred and sixty feet long. They are all of stone, and in a tolerably good state of preservation.

This illustration is a magnificent example of the richness of the Puuc style: we can see the recurrent, and almost obsessive, repetition of the grotesque mask of the god Chac. The figure in the centre showed an unusual throne in the shape of the arc of a circle on which a dignitary or a priest was seated wearing an impressive feather head-dress. Recently there has been much debate whether the Maya had discovered the principle of the arch or if they had been near to discovering it. Looking at this decorative element, a doubt arises: if the "throne" is turned upside down, a proper arch is created, including a perfectly formed keystone. In other words, if the ashlars were mounted the other way up, they would stand perfectly well and it is strange to think that the Mayan architects had never thought of this possibility, particularly as there were very many similar decorative elements in other sites. The Maya were great mathematicians and astronomers and it seems unbelievable that they did not conceive the physical laws underpinning the erection of a round arch. We can only imagine that their choice not to use the arch was dictated by particular aesthetical tastes or by religious limitations, i.e. that curves, being perfect, were the realm of the gods and therefore not for use by mortals.

PLATE X

Archway; Casa del Gobernador, Uxmal

Within about sixty feet of either end of the Casa del Gobernador, are situated the arched gateways, of which one is shown in the drawing. They appear to have been blocked-up by the original builders, as the style of the masonry is precisely similar to that of other parts of the edifice. The triangular arch is distinctly seen, forming the prominent feature of the design. At the angles are hideous masks, one over the other, the projecting trunk, or proboscis, being in the place of the nose. An elegant ornament is carved on either side of the arch, very similar to those found on Greek and Roman buildings. The twisted cable, or rope ornament, is also of frequent occurrence in Yucatan; it is to be found, I believe, in all countries which have made any advance in the art of building. The portion represented in this drawing may be considered as a continuation of the last Plate. They both form a part of the great facade of the Governor's House, and are not less remarkable for their novelty of design, than for their beautiful workmanship.

Once more, Catherwood's attention is concentrated on the most peculiar structure built by the Maya: the false vault. Current theory suggests that the structure was intended to reproduce the internal space of a typical Mesoamerican hut built from wood, plaster and branches. Despite what Catherwood observed, it must be said that the stones that form the intrados are not functional and only hold together thanks to very tenacious mortar used as internal filling. The Mayan vault was not in fact a true vault (in the sense of a balanced system of lateral forces) but neither was it a jutting vault in which the forces are vertical and the stones supported by those beneath. The secret of the Mayan vault lay in the mortar they used which formed a compact and resistant mass when dry although it was susceptible to perpendicular fractures and caving in. This explains why it could not be used to arc over wide spaces.

PLATE XI

GATEWAY OF THE GREAT TEOCALLIS, UXMAL

The great Teocallis at Uxmal is called, by the Indians, the "House of the Diviner," and also the "Dwarf's House." It is a lofty pyramidal mound, about two hundred and thirty-five feet long, by a breadth of one hundred and fifty-five feet. Its height is eighty-eight feet, and to the top of the building, one hundred and five feet. At the height of sixty feet is a solid projecting platform, formerly reached by a steep flight of steps, now thrown down. On this platform stands the gateway represented in the drawing. It measures twenty-two feet in front, and is twenty-two feet high, and was most elaborately adorned with sculptured stone-work. The ornaments are of similar design to those of the Casa del Gobernador, but executed perhaps with a greater degree of delicacy. The remains of two statues are seen, and most likely the niche in the centre was for the reception of a larger one. The doorway is five feet five inches wide, and ten feet high, with lintels of sapote wood still in their places. The interior is divided into two apartments, the outer, fifteen feet long, by seven feet wide, and nineteen feet high; and the inner one, twelve feet long, four feet wide, and eleven feet high. Both are entirely destitute of ornament, and it is not easy to conjecture to what end they served, as they are small, and have no apparent connection with the rest of the building.

The table reproduces the west temple of the Pyramid of the Magician (which Catherwood called "house") built during the fourth phase of the expansion of the structure. It is decorated in Chenes style (earlier than Puuc) with the entrance in the form of a serpent's jaws encircled by two rows of masks of the god Chac.

PLATE XII

ORNAMENT OVER THE GATEWAY OF THE GREAT TEOCALLIS, UXMAL

This elegant specimen of Indian design and workmanship forms part of the front of the upper building of the Diviner's House, mentioned in the preceding description. The edifice is seventy-two feet in length and twelve feet deep. The interior is divided into three apartments, the centre one twenty-four by seven, and the side ones nineteen by seven. These apartments did not communicate with each other; the side ones had each a doorway opening to the eastward, and the middle room a doorway facing the west now destroyed of which the position is shown in the drawing. The ornament is somewhat different in character to that of the other buildings at Uxmal. The relief is low, and, unassisted by bright colours, would hardly have been visible from the ground, even aided by the transparent atmosphere of a tropical climate. There can be little doubt (speaking by analogy) that the entire facade was painted, although all traces of colour have disappeared. The pedestals and remains of eight statues are visible on this facade.

The temple on the summit was part of the last expansion of the Pyramid of the Magician; it was built in Puuc style and has two facades. The side facing east can only be reached by a steep stairway while the side facing west (shown) has two smaller sets of steps which frame the Chenes-style temple seen in the preceding table and reach its terrace.

PLATE XIII

GENERAL VIEW OF UXMAL, TAKEN FROM THE ARCHWAY OF LAS MONJAS, LOOKING SOUTH

This view embraces several of the most remarkable ruins at Uxmal, and the remaining ones are shown by Plate VIII. To the extreme left, in the distance, is the "Casa de la Vieja", or of the "Old Woman", a small teocallis, having at its base the rudely sculptured statue of a woman, from which it derives its name. The second and most colossal terrace of the Casa del Gobernador is seen extending to the right; and in the centre of the view is the casa itself, seen endwise: for a description of it, see Plate IX. Beneath it, and a little to the right, is the "Casa de las Tortugas," or "House of the Turtles:" this name was given to it by Padre Carillo, of Ticul, from a bead, or row, of turtles, which goes entirely round the building on the upper cornice. The length of this edifice is ninety-four feet by a depth of thirty-four, and, in size and ornament, contrasts strikingly with the Casa del Gobernador. It wants the rich and gorgeous decoration of the former, but is distinguished for its justness and beauty of proportion, and its chasteness and simplicity of ornament: unhappily it is fast going to decay. In 1839, it was trembling and tottering, and by 1842, the whole of the centre had fallen in, and the interior was blocked up with the ruins of the fallen roof. Beyond the Casa de las Tortugas are two large teocalli, on the nearest of which are no remains of building, but the furthest has on its summit the ruins of an edifice, somewhat similar in its plan to the structure of the Great Teocallis, or "House of the Diviner". In front of the last building stands the "Casa de Palomos", or "House of the Pigeons": it is two hundred and forty feet long, composed of a double range of rooms, from the dividing wall of which rise pyramidal structures, not unlike the gables of an Elizabethan or Gothic house. The small oblong openings give them somewhat the appearance of pigeon houses, whence the name.

As usual, Catherwood's description is more than exhaustive. We can only add that the two *monticoli* in the foreground were all that remained of the ball-court — an important structure in any Mayan city — and that the "triangular walls", today known as "combs", were a typical decorative element of Mayan architecture. The function of the building is still open to conjecture.

PLATE XIV

PORTION OF THE BUILDING; LAS MONJAS, UXMAL

The engraving represents a portion of the facade, on the left, or western side, entering the court-yard. It was, when entire, one hundred and seventy-three feet long; and is distinguished by two colossal serpents, entwined, running through and encompassing nearly all the ornaments throughout its whole length. Only two portions of this facade now remain; the plate exhibits that towards the north end of the building. The tail of the serpent is held up nearly over its head, and has an ornament upon it like a turban, with a plume of feathers. The marks on the extremity of the tail are probably intended to designate a rattlesnake, with which species of serpent the country abounds. The head of the serpent has its monstrous jaws wide open, and within them is a human head. The other portion remaining shows two entwined serpents, enclosing and running through the ornaments over a doorway. The principal feature in the ornament enclosed, is the figure of a human being, standing, but much mutilated. The bodies of the serpents, according to the representations of the same design in other parts of the sculpture, are covered with feathers. The plate shows about one-tenth of the whole facade; the other nine-tenths were enriched with the same mass of sculptured ornaments; and, towards the south end, the head and tail of the serpents corresponded in design and position with the portion still existing at the other. Don Simian Peon, the proprietor of Uxmal, said, that in 1835 the whole front stood perfect, and serpents were seen encircling every ornament in the building. These have since fallen, and lie in confused heaps at the foot of the monument.

PLATE XV

PORTION OF LA CASA DE LAS MONJAS, UXMAL

This section forms part of an exceedingly rich and highly-decorated facade, two hundred and sixty-four feet long; and which, for profusion of ornament, rivals, if it does not surpass, the front of the Casa del Gobernador. It is useless attempting to explain by words that which is so much more perfectly understood by inspection of the drawing. The only remark perhaps necessary is this: there is, or rather were, five similar structures in the facade, and, although at a distance, they appear exactly alike and are so, as regards general outline and size yet the detail and making up of the ornaments differ in each; and this observation will apply equally to the facades of nearly all the buildings at Uxmal, in which occur endless varieties in the detail of the decorations.

PLATE XVI

GENERAL VIEW OF KABAH

The view of Kabah is almost perfect except for the exaggerated size of the pyramid seen on the left. Nevertheless, the error can be attributed to the fact that the structure was still covered by a thick and leafy layer of trees. The scene in the foreground refers to the transportation of a magnificently carved, wooden architrave found at a site near Kabah. Stephens intended to take the architrave back to New York with him. Unfortunately the precious find has been lost.

The ruins of Kabah lie on the common lands of the village of Nohcacab. Perhaps they have been known to the Indians from time immemorial; but, as we were informed by the Padre of the village of Nohcacab, until the opening of the road to Bolonchen, they were utterly unknown to the white inhabitants. This road passed through the ancient city, and revealed the great buildings, overgrown and, in some cases, towering above the tops of the trees. The discovery, however, created not the slightest sensation; the intelligence of it had never reached the capital; and though, ever since its occurrence, the great edifices were visible to all who passed along the road, not a white man in the village had ever turned aside to look at them, except the Padre referred to. The Teocallis, to the left of the drawing, is the first object that meets the eye; grand, picturesque, ruined, and covered with trees, towering above every other object on the plain. Leaving this, and following a path to the distance of three or four hundred yards, we reach the foot of a terrace, twenty feet high, the edge of which is overgrown with trees; ascending this, we stand on a platform, two hundred feet in width, by one hundred and forty-two feet deep. In the centre of the platform is a range of stone steps, forty feet wide and twenty in number, leading to an upper terrace. On this terrace stands a building, on the extreme right of the drawing, one hundred and fifty-one feet in front, remarkable for the extraordinary richness and ornament of its facade. In all the buildings of Uxmal, without a single exception, up to the cornice which runs over the doorway, the buildings are plain stone, but this was ornamented from the very foundation, two layers under the lower cornice, to the top. The ornaments are of the same character with those at Uxmal, alike complicated

and incomprehensible. The cornice running over the doorway is very elegant and graceful in its design, and would not disgrace the architecture of a more polished people.

This building has five doorways in front, communicating to as many outer rooms; and these again to five other inner rooms, entirely dark, except the light which enters through the doorways. Windows are not found in the Yucatan buildings, but there is an occasional substitute for them, in small narrow openings, four or five inches wide and twelve inches high, admitting a little light and air.

The Casa, or building, next the last-mentioned, stands on a platform, one hundred and seventy feet long, by one hundred and ten feet broad. It consists of two stories, the lower one almost entirely ruined. The chambers are very small, with doorways opening on to the platform. A little to the right in the drawing is a Teocallis, measuring one hundred and forty feet on one side, and one hundred and six on the other. It consists of three distinct stories, each receding from, and being smaller than, the one under, and terminating with a broad platform on the top, with a handsome stone staircase on each side.

In the distance is seen a building, called by the Indians "Casa de la Justicia," or House of Justice. It measures one hundred and thirteen feet in front, and has five chambers, each twenty feet long and nine feet wide, and all perfectly plain. The exterior is slightly ornamented. At the foot of the Teocallis is a solitary arch, fourteen feet in the opening, and constructed after the peculiar fashion of the country. From its position, it would seem to have been one of the main entrances into the city, or, possibly, a commemorative triumphal arch.

PLATE XVII

INTERIOR OF THE PRINCIPAL BUILDING AT KABAH

The exterior of this building is described at the preceding Plate. The interior consists of two parallel chambers, the one in front being twenty-seven feet long and ten feet six inches wide; and the other of the same length, but a few inches narrower, communicating by a doorway in the centre. The inner room is raised two feet eight inches higher than the front, and the ascent is by two steps, carved out of a single block of stone, the lower one (see Drawing) being in the form of a scroll. The sides of the steps are enriched with a similar ornament to that of the facade of the building. Extending from either side of this ornament to the ends of the apartment are small engaged columns, without either base or capital. The whole composition is graceful and pretty, and the scroll step in particular is one of the most appropriate designs to be met with in Yucatan.

From Catherwood's description it is clear how interpretation of many figurative elements was extremely difficult without an adequate knowledge of the expressive language of the Maya or of their complex religious pantheon. The "decorative motif" and the two "sets of steps" are no more than a mask of the god Chac, lord of the rain, whose unusual feature is his long, curled nose.

PLATE XVIII

WELL AND BUILDING AT SABACHTSCHÉ

The Rancho of Sabachtsché lies on the Camino Real from Ticul to Bolonchen. It is inhabited entirely by Indians, and is distinguished by a well, built by the present proprietor of the Rancho. Formerly the inhabitants were dependent entirely upon the well at Tabi, six miles distant. Besides its real value, this well presented a curious and lively spectacle. A group of women was around. It had no rope or fixtures of any kind for raising water, but across the mouth was a round beam, laid upon two posts, over which the women were letting down and hoisting up little bark buckets . Every woman brought with her, and carried away, her own bucket and rope, the latter coiled up and laid on the top of her head, with the end hanging down behind, and forming a sort of head-dress. The building which appears in the engraving, stands in the suburbs of the Rancho, just beyond the huts of the Indians. We found it overgrown by trees, and beautifully picturesque. On one corner of the roof a vulture had built her nest, and, scared away at our approach, hovered over our heads, looking down upon us. The front of this building appeared tasteful, and even elegant in design, and, when perfect, it must have presented a fine appearance. It has a single doorway, opening into a chamber twenty-five feet long, by ten feet wide. Above the door is a portion of plain masonry, and over this a cornice, supporting twelve small pilasters, having between them a diamond ornament; then a massive cornice, with pilasters and diamond work, surmounted by another cornice, making in all four cornices, an arrangement we had not previously met with.

PLATE XIX

GATEWAY AT LABNÁ

This may be considered as one of the most pleasing architectural designs to be met with among the ruined edifices of Yucatan. It is the inner facade of an arched gateway, ten feet wide, leading into what was formerly the court-yard of a large building. Under the arch are two doorways, giving entrance to two small rooms, twelve feet by eight, which also have openings towards the area. Over each doorway is a square recess, flanked by small pilasters, and supporting a mass of masonry pyramidally disposed. In the recesses are the remains of rich ornaments in stucco, with marks of colours still clearly visible, perhaps intended to represent the face of the sun surrounded by its rays, and probably to the Indian an object of superstitious adoration. The construction of the arch is the same as is found all over the country. The stones are laid horizontally, each projecting a little beyond the under one, until at last they nearly meet, and a flat cover-stone completes the arch, if it may be so called. This species of roof has its advantages; there is no lateral thrust, and frequently when one side of an apartment, and, consequently, half the roof had fallen, the other remains entire. The cement used was very good, equal, in many instances, to that found in the ancient Roman buildings.

The comment relating to Table XVII is also valid here: the strange frieze described by Catherwood is in fact the stylisation of a typical Mayan house. The Englishman had visited a land that was by then widely influenced by the culture introduced by the European conquistadors, in which the indigenous inhabitants had assumed different customs to those of the past and lived in houses that were very different to those of their forebears. Only in relatively recent times have scholars been able to interpret the ornamental motifs of the arch of Labná which are of great importance for our understanding of Mayan house structures. The "deity", of which no trace remains, was in fact a richly dressed priest or a dignitary.

PLATE XX

WELL AT BOLONCHEN

Bolonchen derives its name from two Maya words, Bolon, which signifies "nine," and Chen, "wells;" and it means "the nine wells." From time immemorial, nine wells formed at this place the centre of a population, and these are now in the plaza of the village. Their origin is as obscure and unknown as that of the ruined cities which strew the land, and as little thought of.

The custody and supply of these wells form a principal part of the business of the village authorities, but with all their care the supply of water lasts but seven or eight months in the year. At the period of our visit the time was approaching when the wells would fail, and the inhabitants be driven to an extraordinary cavern, at half a league's distance from the village.

There was one grand difficulty in the way of our visiting the cavern, or well. Since the commencement of the rainy season it had not been used; and every year, before having recourse to it, there was a work of several days to be done in repairing the ladders.

Setting out, however, from the village of Bolonchen, by the Campeachy road, we turned off by a well beaten path, following which we fell into a winding lane, and, descending gradually, reached the foot of the rude, lofty, and abrupt opening, under a bold ledge of overhanging rock, seeming a magnificent entrance to a great temple for the worship of the God of nature.

We disencumbered ourselves of superfluous apparel, and following the Indians, each with a torch in his hand, entered a wild cavern, which, as we advanced, became darker. At the distance of sixty paces the descent was precipitous, and we went down by a ladder about twenty feet. Here all light from the mouth of the cavern was lost,

but we soon reached the brink of a great perpendicular descent, to the very bottom of which a strong body of light was thrown from a hole in the surface; a perpendicular depth, as we afterwards found by measurement, of two hundred and ten feet. As we stood on the brink of this precipice, under the shelving of an immense mass of rock, seeming darker from the stream of light thrown down the hole, gigantic stalactites and huge blocks of stones assumed all manner of fantastic shapes, and seemed like monstrous animals or deities of a subterraneous world.

From the brink on which we stood, an enormous ladder of the rudest possible construction led to the bottom of the hole. It was between seventy and eight feet long, and about twelve feet wide, made of the rough trunks of saplings lashed together lengthways, and supported all the way down by horizontal trunks braced against the face of the precipitous rock. The ladder was double, having two sets, or flights, of rounds, divided by a middle partition, and the whole fabric was lashed together by withes. It was very steep, seemed precarious and insecure, and confirmed the worst accounts we had heard of the descent into this extraordinary well.

Our Indians began the descent, but the foremost had hardly got his head below the surface, before one of the rounds broke, and he only saved himself by clinging to another. The ladder having been made when the withes were green, there were now dry, cracked, and some of them broken. We attempted a descent with some little misgivings; but by keeping each hand and foot on a different round, with an occasional crash and slide, we all reached the foot of the ladder; that is, our own party, our Indians, and some three or four of our escort, the rest having disappeared. Plate

XX. represents the scene at the foot of this ladder. Looking up, the view of its broken sides, with the light thrown down from the orifice above, was the wildest that can be conceived. As yet we were only at the mouth of this well, called by the Indians, "La Senora escondida;" or, "the Lady hidden away:" and it is derived from a fanciful Indian story, that a lady, stolen from her mother, was concealed by her lover in this cave. On one side of the cavern is an opening in the rock, entering by which, we soon came to an abrupt descent, down which was another long and trying ladder. It was laid against the broken face of the rock, not so steep as the first, but in a much more rickety condition: the rounds were loose, and the upper ones gave way on the first attempt to descend. The cave was damp, and the rock and the ladder were wet and slippery. It was evident that the labour of exploring this cave was to be greatly increased by the state of the ladders, and there might be some danger attending it; but, even after all we had seen of caves, there was something so wild and grand in this that we could not bring ourselves to give up the attempt. Fortunately, the Cura had taken care to provide us with a rope, and fastening one end round a large stone, an Indian carried the other down to the foot of the ladder. We followed one at a time; holding the rope with one hand, and with other grasping the side of the ladder: it was impossible to carry a torch, and we were obliged to feel our way in the dark, or with only such light as could reach us from the torches above and below. At the foot of this ladder was a large cavernous chamber, with irregular passages branching off in different directions to seven deposite or sources of water, from which the village of Bolonchen is supplied.

PLATE XXI

LAS MONJAS, CHICHÉN ITZÁ

The plate represents the end facade of a long majestic pile, called, like one of the principal buildings at Uxmal, the "Monjas," or "Nuns." The height of this facade is twenty-five feet, and its width thirty-five. It has two cornices of tasteful design; over the doorway are twenty small cartouches of hieroglyphics, in four rows, five in a row, and to make room for which the lower cornice is carried up; over them stand out, in a line, six bold projecting curved ornaments, resembling an elephant's trunk; and the upper centre space over the doorway is an irregular circular niche, in which portions of a seated figure, with a head-dress of feathers, still remain. The rest of the ornaments are of that distinctive stamp, characteristic of the ancient American cities, and unlike the designs of any other people. The building is composed of two structures, entirely different from each other; one of which forms a sort of wing to the principal edifice, and has at the end the facade presented. The whole length is two hundred and twenty-eight feet, and the depth of the principal structure is one hundred and twelve feet.

The only portion containing interior chambers is that which we have called the wing. The great structure to which the wing adjoins is apparently a solid mass of masonry, erected only to hold up the two ranges of buildings upon it. A grand staircase, fifty-six feet wide, the largest we saw in the country, runs to the top. This staircase is thirty-two feet high, and has thirty-nine steps. On the top of the structure stands a range of buildings, with a platform of fourteen feet in front, extending all around. From the back of this platform the grand staircase rises again, by fifteen steps, to the roof of the second range, which forms a platform in front of the third range. The circumference of this building is six hundred and thirty-eight feet, and its height, when entire, was sixty-five feet. The art and skill of the builders seem to have been lavishly expended upon the second range: this is one hundred and four feet long and thirty feet wide; and the broad platform around it, though overgrown with grass several feet high, formed a noble promenade, commanding a magnificent view of the whole surrounding country.

Chichén Itzá was a large centre that flourished between the 9th and 10th centuries AD. It contains some of the most elegant Mayan monuments. The Nunnery, so called by its discoverers for its resemblance to a convent, is a masterpiece of Puuc art. The abundance of decoration does not hide the functional purity of the architectural lines (as, for example, at Kabah) giving a pleasing impression overall. What Catherwood called "hieroglyphs" are know by modern archaeology as glyphs – the characters of Mayan writing – which have mostly been deciphered in recent years. It is obvious that the English artist had understood the real nature of the signs which many of his contemporaries had considered as simple ornamental elements.

PLATE XXII

Teocallis, at Chichén Itzá

The ruins of Chichen-Itza are nine leagues from Valladolid. (See Map.) They lie on a Hacienda, called by the name of the ancient city.

The Camino Real to Valladolid passes through the field of ruins. The great buildings tower on both sides of the road in full sight of all passers-by; and from the fact that this road is much travelled, the ruins of Chichen are perhaps more generally known to the people of the country than any others in Yucatan. The Plate represents the Castillo, or Castle, the first building seen on approaching the ruins, and, from every point of view, the grandest and most conspicuous object that towers above the plain. The mound measures at the base, on the north and south sides, one hundred and ninety-six feet ten inches; and on the east and west sides, two hundred and two feet. It does not face the cardinal points exactly, though probably so intended; and in all the buildings, from some cause not easily accounted for, while one varies ten degrees one way, that immediately adjoining varies twelve or thirteen degrees the other. It is built up, apparently solid, from the plain to the height of seventy-five feet. On the west side is a staircase, thirty-seven feet wide; on the north, being that presented in the engraving, the staircase is forty-four feet wide, and has ninety steps. On the ground at the foot of the staircase, forming a bold, striking, and well-conceived commencement to this lofty range, are two colossal serpent's heads, ten feet in length, with mouths wide open and tongues protruding, as shown by the fragment in the foreground of the drawing: no doubt they were emblematic of some religious belief.

The platform on the top of the mound measures sixty-one feet from north to south, and sixty-four from east to west; and the building measures, in the same directions, forty-three feet and forty-nine. Single doorways face the east, south, and west, having massive lintels of sapote wood covered with elaborate carvings, and the stone jambs are ornamented with figures. The sculpture is much worn; but the head-dresses, ornamented with plumes of feathers, and portions of the rich attire, still remain. The face of one of the figures is well preserved, and has a dignified appearance; it has, too, earrings, and the nose bored, which, according to historical account, was so prevalent a custom in Yucatan, that long after the conquest the Spaniards passed laws for its prohibition.

All the other jambs are decorated with sculpture of the same general character; and all open into a corridor six feet wide, extending round three sides of the building.

The doorway facing the north, represented in the engraving, presents a grander appearance, being twenty feet wide, and having two short massive columns, eight feet eight inches high, with two large projections at the base, entirely covered with elaborate sculpture. This doorway gives access to a corridor forty feet long by six feet four inches wide and seventeen feet high. In the back wall of this corridor is a single doorway, having sculptured jambs, over which is a richly-carved sapote beam, and giving entrance to an apartment nineteen feet eight inches long, twelve feet nine inches wide, and seventeen feet high. In this apartment are two square pillars, nine feet four inches high and one foot ten inches on each side, having sculptured figures on all their sides, and supporting massive sapote beams, covered with the most elaborate carving of curious and intricate designs, but so defaced and time-worn, that, in the obscurity of the room, lighted only from the door, it was difficult to make them out. The impression produced on entering this lofty chamber, so entirely different from all we had met with before, was perhaps stronger than any we had yet experienced. We passed a whole day within it, from time to time looking down upon the ruined buildings of the ancient city, and an immense field stretching on all sides beyond.

Excellent observer as he was, Catherwood noted some anomalies in the orientation of many Mayan buildings though he did not find an explanation. Only many years later was it discovered that the palaces and pyramids were actually astronomical observatories, not necessarily directed at the points of the compass but angled to sight particular stars, constellations and planets. The Mayan astronomers had a deep knowledge of the movements of the sun, moon, Mercury, Venus, Mars, Jupiter and, probably, Saturn. They also knew the movements of the constellations along the ecliptic and considered the Pole Star extremely important for its use in guiding travellers and merchants.

With regard to the Castillo, each ramp that flanks the northern steps of the pyramid forms the stylised body of a snake whose head rests on the ground. As Catherwood had correctly understood, they are strongly symbolic: they represent Quetzalcoatl, the mythical Plumed Serpent worshipped by the Toltecs and imported to the Maya when the Toltecs invaded the Yucatán from central Mexico. The English artist could not have imagined how much archeologists would discover about this structure; this 13th-century pyramid contains a smaller version inside that is older by about two centuries.

PLATE XXIII

CASTLE, AT TULÚM

The ruined City of Tuloom is situated on a ledge of rocks on the eastern shore of Yucatan. The building given in Plate XXIII., although called a Castillo, or Castle, was, there can be little doubt, a place used for the religious ceremonies of the Indians. At the time the drawing was made, trees obstructed the view, which had to be cut down before the design of the edifice could be made out. The building, including the wings, measures at its base one hundred feet in length. The grand staircase is thirty feet wide, with twenty-four steps; and a substantial parapet on each side—still in good preservation gives it an unusually imposing character. In the doorway are two columns, making three entrances, with square recesses above them, all of which once contained ornaments; and in the centre, and one of the side ones, fragments of statues still remain. The interior is divided into two corridors, each twenty-six feet long; the one in front is six feet six inches wide, and had at each end a stone bench or divan. A single doorway leads to the back and copal, making it probable that some Indians had recently been engaged in celebrating their ancient religious rites, which they still adhere to when not within observation of the Spaniards. On each side of the doorway are stone rings, intended for the support of the door, and in the back wall are oblong openings, which admit breezes from the sea. Both apartments have the triangular arched ceiling, and both were conveniently and pleasantly arranged for living apartments. The wings are much lower than the principal building. Each consists of two ranges; the under one standing on a low platform, from which are steps leading to the upper. The latter consists of two chambers, of which the one in front is twenty-four feet long and twenty wide, having two columns in the doorway, and two in the middle of the chamber. The centre columns were ornamented with devices in stucco, one of which was a masked face, and the other the head of a rabbit. The walls were entire, but the roof had fallen; the rubbish on the floor was less massive then that formed in other places by the remains of the triangular arched roof, and of different materials; and there were holes along the top of the wall, as if beams had been laid in them, all of which induced the belief that the roofs had been flat, and supported by wooden beams resting on the two columns in the centre. From this apartment a doorway, three feet wide, close to the wall of the principal building, leads to a chamber twenty-four feet long and nine feet wide, also roofless, and having the same indications that the roof had been flat and supported by wooden beams; which opinion was afterwards verified, by the discovery of wooden roofs still entire in the adjoining buildings.

What Catherwood called "corridors" due to their long and narrow appearance were actually quite common in Mayan architecture and are only rooms that, from a European point of view, have an unusual shape. Their peculiar form is created by the constant use of the false vault which, for static and dynamic reasons, is not suitable for covering wide spaces whereas it can be stretched lengthways indefinitely.

PLATE XXIV

TEMPLE, AT TULÚM

The Temple at Tuloom faces
towards the east, and is distant two
hundred and fifty feet from the
Castillo, or Castle, described in the last
plate. Although the distance is but
trifling, the whole area is so blocked up
with trees, that it was by mere accident
this building and several others were
discovered. It stands on a terrace six
feet high, with a staircase in the centre.
The front of the building measures
forty-five feet by a depth of twenty-
six. There are two stout pillars still
standing in the principal doorway,
supporting wooden beams; and over the
centre are the remains of a head,
surrounded by a profusion of feathers.
The interior is divided into two
principal and parallel apartments; and
at the north extremity of the inner one
is a smaller chamber, containing an
enclosed altar five feet long by three feet
six inches deep, for burning copal. The
roof had fallen, and trees were growing
out of the floor.

The table needs no comment: it shows the
enormous amount of work needed to free
the Mayan temples from the embrace of
the vegetation. This is the only illustration
in which Catherwood has shown himself.
It is generally thought that the person on
the right is Catherwood and the one on
the left Stephens.

PLATE XXV

COLOSSAL HEAD, AT IZAMAL

Izamal, at the height of its prosperity, must have been one of the most important of the Indian cities of Yucatan. There is abundant testimony to prove that it was inhabited at the time of the Spanish conquest. There are still remaining several mounds, one of which is the largest in Yucatan, but so dilapidated and disfigured, as to defy accurate measurement: it may be about seven hundred feet long and sixty high. It is said to contain interior chambers and colossal statues; but no entrance at present exists to these subterranean apartments. The great church and convent of the Franciscan monks stands on the upper platform of one of the ancient teocalli, and the open area fronting the church is probably not less than two hundred feet square, surrounded on three sides by an open colonnade, forming a noble promenade, overlooking the modern city of Izamal and the surrounding country to a great distance. On the side of a mound about two hundred feet long, and which formerly had stone and stucco ornaments from one end to the other, is the Colossal Head perhaps of some deity represented in the plate: it is seven feet eight inches in height, and seven feet in width. A stone, one foot six inches long, protrudes from the chin, intended perhaps for burning copal on.

Catherwood indulges in a certain degree of romanticism but, in doing so, falls into a large error as jaguars do not actually inhabit the forests of northern Yucatán. Nonetheless, the documentary value of the table is remarkable as the mask shown, like most of the large Mayan buildings at Izamál, has been destroyed, swallowed up by the development of the colonial city founded by the Spanish on the ruins of a much older centre.

GULF OF

MEXICO

YUCATAN

Sisal

Merida

UXMAL

COZUMEL

o Campeachy

BAY OF

HONDURAS

TABASCO

Palisada

Playes
Village of Palenque
PALENQUE

Tumbala

LAKE OF
TERMINOS

Lake of Peten

BRITISH SETTLEMENT

BALIZE

MEXICO

Ciudad Real
or S.t Christobal

Rio del Lagarto

OCOSINGO

CHIAPAS

COMITAN

Guista

ROATAN

Carib Village

OMOA

Gueguetenango

GOLFO DULCE

HONDURAS

HONDUR

QUEZALTENANGO

S.t CRUZ DEL
QUICHE

Salama

S.t Thomas

Totonicapan

Solola

Lake of Atitlan

GUAT

Misco

MALA

Metagua River

Iscapa

Zacapa

Chiquimula

Gualan

QUIRIGUA

Encuentros

COPAN

El Fuerte

El Guilgolpa

Guatemala

Old Guatemala

Chichicastenango

Amatitlan

Escuintla

Esquipulas

Port of Istapa

Acazalu

Jocotepeque

S.t Salvador

S.t Vicente

SONSONATE

La Tusma

S.t Michel

S.t SALVADOR

Volcano of
Cosiguina

Nagascols

PACIFIC

NICA

Realejo

LAKE OF LEON

LEON

OCEAN

Managua

GRENADA

LAKE
of NIC

Port of S.t Juan
GULF of
PAPAGATO

Bagason

Cape

MAP
OF JOURNEY IN
CENTRAL AMERICA,
CHIAPAS & YUCATAN.

Meridian of Greenwich
The dotted line shows the route taken.

THE FIRST EXPEDITION TO CENTRAL AMERICA

Finally, Catherwood and Stephens left New York on 3 October 1839 on board the brig "Mary Ann". Their destination was British Honduras, the only means of access to the region that they intended to explore. The Englishman, who had perfected his organisational abilities during his trips around Egypt, had with him a complete surveyor's set of equipment and stacks of drawing paper, pencils, pens, drawing ink, his light chamber and the pistol. The American had two revolvers, a good machete, mosquito nets, a collection of government credentials and a large supply of cigars. As soon as they were away from New York, Stephens opened a letter handed to him by the wife of a diplomat, Charles de Witt, who had died of malaria following a mission in Central America. The letter concluded with the rather discouraging words, "I hope you have more fortune than your predecessors".

In an atmosphere that was vaguely worrying but full of excitement, the two disembarked a month later in Belize, an incredibly dirty and unwelcoming place despite the cordiality of the inhabitants. The city had only existed for 150 years or so in Haulover Creek on the Caribbean coast for the trade in mahogany. It was a disordered and smelly jumble of waterside dwellings connected by a network of muddy roads in which naked children played and dirty pigs rooted. The coast of the country was lined with lagoons as far as the eye could see and fronted by rocks surrounded by formations of madrepore. The weather was hot and humid, the air infested with clouds of insects and the inland a green impassable mass lashed with frequent storms. A mysterious land stretched out in front of them, dotted with

villages dating from the Spanish conquest and covered with unexplored jungle. The population of Belize was for the most part black or mestizo, descended from the African slaves brought in chains to the New World by the Spanish. Stephens, who came from a nation where racial segregation was used in places, a nation that would have to fight a civil war and wait twenty four more years to abolish slavery, was amazed to see whites and blacks living side by side. "The town seemed in the entire possession of the blacks... They were a fine-looking race, tall, straight, and athletic, with black, smooth skin, and glossy as velvet, and well dressed... I hardly knew whether to be shocked or amused at this condition of society...".

Soon after their arrival they found a place to stay the night, then received an invitation via the American consul from Colonel MacDonald,

Page 108 – Map of Central America and the route followed by Stephens and Catherwood.

Page 109 – Fragment of sculpture, Copán.

Catherwood D

superintendent of the only British colony in Central America as well as being responsible for the political life of the entire region. After an official lunch, the imposing and pompous colonel, who had fought Napoleon at Waterloo, solemnly promised the two explorers that they would have all his support in case of danger, as the land of the Maya was not considered safe and contained numerous perils. This was a euphemism at best since the area was no more than a time-bomb waiting to go off in which there were continual massacres and killings. The Federation of the United Provinces of Central America, which had been formed by Honduras, Nicaragua, Costa Rica, Salvador and Guatemala in 1824 after independence from Spain, had disintegrated the year

before as a result of local nationalistic forces while the racial antagonism between the white and indigenous populations was growing increasingly violent. The struggle between the factions was obviously abetting foreign interests, in particular Britain's. MacDonald was a patent example of such interference as well as being a master of the double-cross for, while he was promising help, the colonel was manoeuvring so that two of his men, Patrick Walker and lieutenant John Caddy, would achieve the same task first. Caddy and Walker left Belize on 13 November 1839 and reached Palenque about ten weeks later. They carried out a superficial cataloguing of the buildings overgrown with mangroves and Caddy made drawings of the

various monuments and inscriptions found among the ruins even if in a rather flat style. When they returned to Belize on 5 April 1840, they claimed triumphantly that, on the basis of their observations, it could be claimed without any doubt at all that the mysterious Mesoamerican cities could not have been built by local peoples but by Asiatic colonisers or, more exactly, "Indo-Egyptians". Completely forgotten by their contemporaries, their expedition report saw the light of day once more in 1967 when it was found by scholar David Pendergast.

Unaware of the underhand manoeuvres carried out so that an American could not surpass the scientific achievements of a subject of Her Royal Majesty, Stephens and

Catherwood left the miserable city accompanied by a French servant named Augustin whose face had been slashed by a machete and who was diabolically cunning. Their means of transport was a paddle steamer, the *Vera Paz*: they headed south down the Rio Dulce from where they reached Lake Yzabal. Although tortuous, this was an obligatory route as there were no other means of communication between the coast and the inland. The surrounding forest seemed particularly quiet and the only creatures they saw were pelicans, probably disturbed by the noise of the steamer's boilers which Stephens hated with all his heart. Both had travelled far and wide but neither had ever seen such luxuriant vegetation before. In

the village of Yzabal where the steamer finally stopped, they had their first direct experience with the insalubrity of the region when the English engineer of the *Vera Cruz* fell ill with malaria. Catherwood certainly had no idea he would one day suffer the same misfortune. Stephens, meanwhile, had visited the grave of his compatriot, James Shannon, also American chargé d'affaires to Central America, who had died some years before in this godforsaken place. The tomb was squalid and poor Stephens was forced to ponder that three other of his predecessors had fallen to the same fate far from home.

The path that led over Mount Mico and into the heart of the jungle left from the small village on the shores of the crystal clear lake. Stephens, Catherwood and Augustin loaded their victuals and equipment onto mules and headed off towards the unknown with four Indian escorts. There was little to be cheerful about. Guatemala, the borders of which they were about to cross, was in the hands of Carrera, an Indian that was conducting a no holds barred war against Morazan, the white ruler of Salvador, and the mulatto Ferrera, ruler of Honduras. These latter two had only recently met in battle near San Salvador and now Morazan was moving against Guatemala with his bands of bloodthirsty cut-throats. Don Juan Peñol, the commander of the port of Yzabal, had warned

Stephens not to place any reliance on his diplomatic immunity and added that the pass he had just been given would have little value if they came into contact with Morazan's men. It is evident that the two explorers wished to reach Copán in the shortest time possible as the Mayan city was not situated in the theatre of operations.

Armed with a pistol and a sword, Augustin headed the party along an increasingly muddy and steep path. To make progress even more difficult, they had to cope with the deep shade produced by the thick vegetation overhead, the enormous tree roots and the holes in the ground filled with water from the storms of the last few days. In short, no-one had much to say and the group fell into a profound silence. The mules tripped and fell continuously, the insects gave them no peace and the mud had transformed them into grotesque parodies of mounts and riders. The jungle, overarched by gigantic mahogany trees, got even thicker; it was a surreal universe consisting of dripping leaves, extraordinary flowers, enormous butterflies, tree toads and snakes that would undoubtedly have fascinated a biologist but not two travellers wanting only to shine light onto ancient civilisations.

Depressed by Shannon's grave, Stephens thought that their epitaph would sound inglorious: "Tossed over the head of a mule, brained by the trunk of a mahogany tree, and buried in the mud of the Mico Mountains".

Pages 110-111 – View of the upper part of House I, now known as the Pyramid of the Inscriptions, Palenque.

Page 111 – Stucco bas-relief, Palenque

F. Catherwood

S.H. Gimber

A little later and quite unexpectedly, Catherwood was thrown out of the saddle with such force that his companion was petrified with horror for some seconds, convinced Catherwood was dead. As this was not the case, however when Frederick recovered from the blow, he gave Stephens a tongue lashing saying that if he had ever known of this mountain beforehand, Stephens would have had to come to Central America alone. For once, Frederick had lost his aplomb. A moment later and Augustin was thrown to the ground.

In the middle of this daylight nightmare, the group came across a rather absurd figure. Tall, dressed in a muddy poncho and wearing a wide-brimmed Panama hat, he brandished an enormous machete in his right hand and huge spurs jangled on his boots. The apparition bowed and, in perfect English that left them astonished, explained that he was a British gentleman coming from Nueva Guatemala where he had been a bank manager for the past two years and that now he was trying to return home with a bagful of shares. In the presence of such a figure, Catherwood and Stephens must have thought they were not the only madmen in that region after all.

On the second day, the group finally exited the forest and entered an area of highlands surrounded by snow-capped mountains and dotted with gigantic cactuses and mimosa bushes. The march continued through the villages of El Pozo, Enquentros and Gualan that were no more than a handful of adobe houses with straw roofs. Stephens' diplomatic mission was to track down any government in Central America, for which purpose he first had to head directly for

Nueva Guatemala. Nonetheless, his plans were slightly different and first he intended to visit the ruins of Copán that he had read so much about in the accounts of Juan Galindo and Domingo Juarros.

They travelled through the valley of the river Motagua as far as Zacapa where they turned south towards Chiquimula situated in the middle of corn fields, banana plantations and rows of prickly pear cactus plants. The local people were friendly and offered their hospitality so that Catherwood and Stephens never had to suffer hunger despite losing many of their provisions when they were accidentally mixed with gunpowder. The diet of tortillas and beans, though, was rather monotonous. The only real discomfort was the sun but even this provided an attraction, though somewhat embarrassing for two gentlemen: to cope with the heat, the clothes of the local women were rather scanty and it is easy to imagine how wide Stephens' and Catherwood's eyes must have opened in admiration. The pages of the American's diary contained many appreciations of the raven-haired young girls they met on the roads though he never managed to accept the passion they had for cigars. All went well until they entered the tiny village of Comatán which was no more than a bunch of small houses around a church with the usual dazzling white plastered facade. Here they were taken prisoner by a group of armed bandits – Indians, whites and mestizos – who took their orders from a young "officer" in the pay of General Cascara, one of General Carrera's allies. He wanted to see the personal documents of the two

foreigners but he understood so little that he decided to ask for instructions from his superior. The General was at that moment in Chiquimula and the group would therefore have had to remain holed up in their hovel for an unknown period. Stephens flew into a temper but this achieved nothing, so Catherwood decided to intervene with all his British phlegm, treating his amazed audience to a dignified lecture on "the law of nations, the right of an ambassador, and the danger of bringing down upon them the

vengeance of the government del Norte". But even this eloquent speech did not untangle the situation which was only resolved a day later with the arrival of an older officer who allowed the two to send a letter to Cascara. Stephens dictated the text and Frederick translated it into Italian – the General's mother tongue – signing it as the "secretary" of the American ambassador. In place of an official stamp, the wax was sealed with a new half dollar. Several hours later, they were finally allowed to proceed.

Once they had left this ugly episode behind them, Stephens and Catherwood had to march for two more days, cross the Copán river several times and climb a few hills before reaching their longed for destination on 13 November. Their troubles, though, were not ended. The village of Copán was no more than "half a dozen miserable huts" and the hacienda of Don Gregorio, a man they found impossible to deal with. Irate, vulgar, coarse and ignorant of the most basic elements of hospitality, this cantankerous person with a coal black moustache was, unfortunately, one of the most powerful people in the area and he was not at all keen on the foreigners. Not only did he not like their appearance, he disliked the Italian accent Catherwood used when he spoke Spanish, nor was he keen on being spoken to in French by Augustin. Since these characters who had appeared from nowhere were more than likely spies, Don Gregorio refused to give them any information on the ruins or let his men help them, even as a guide. With this fresh wave of hostility, and offended by the manner in which they were treated, Stephens was ready to explode but once again his quiet assistant intervened. In the book Incidents of Travel, Stephens describes and mentions his companion infrequently but, although taciturn, Catherwood must have been a good travel companion. From the few notes on the subject, a figure, with a certain character, emerges as well as an excellent practical sense that was able to temper the angry outbursts of the American and reason with him. In this difficult situation with Don Gregorio too, Frederick succeeded in calming Stephens and suggested

greater diplomacy. This must have had the desired effect as Don Gregorio, perhaps scared of attracting the ire of the pair's mysterious allies, disappeared the next day and one of his sons found them a guide named José. In a short time, José cut a path through the jungle with his machete to the river Copán and on the other side they saw "a stone wall, perhaps a hundred feet high, with furze growing out of the top, running north and south along the river". Stephens did not realise the nature of the ruin, which was in fact a section of the

Acropolis undermined by the river, and believed it was a wall to protect the city. Anyway, he understood he had entered on virgin territory and that he was close to opening a new chapter in the study of American civilisations. He was right. That moment was of supreme importance, not only for the knowledge of Copán, but of the entire Mayan civilisation.

José found a ford where they crossed the river. Hacking with his machete, he led them through the massive ruins buried beneath the luxuriant vegetation. The only

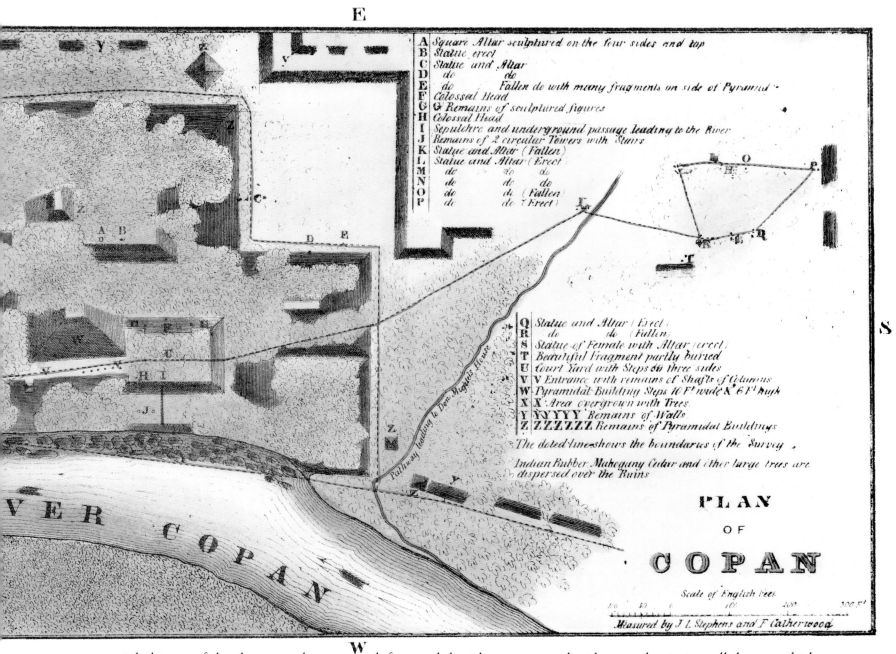

E

A	Square Altar sculptured on the four sides and top
B	Statue erect
C	Statue and Altar
D	do do
E	do Fallen do with many fragments on side of Pyramid
F	Colossal Head
G	Remains of sculptured figures
H	Colossal Head
I	Sepulchre and underground passage leading to the River
J	Remains of 2 circular Towers with Stairs
K	Statue and Altar (Fallen)
L	Statue and Altar (Erect)
M	do do do
N	do do do
O	do do (Fallen)
P	do do (Erect)

Q	Statue and Altar (Erect)
R	do do (Fallen)
S	Statue of Female with Altar (erect)
T	Beautiful Fragment partly buried
U	Court Yard with Steps on three sides
V	Entrance with remains of Shafts of Columns
W	Pyramidal Building Steps 10 Ft wide & 6 Ft high
X	Area overgrown with Trees
Y	YYYYY Remains of Walls
Z	ZZZZZZ Remains of Pyramidal Buildings

The dotted line shows the boundaries of the Survey.

Indian Rubber Mahogany Cedar and other large trees are dispersed over the Ruins

RIVER COPAN

PLAN
OF
COPAN

Scale of English Feet.

Measured by J L Stephens and F Catherwood

inhabitants of the place were the monkeys that screeched in fright at their intrusion. In the green, almost liquid light of the undergrowth, Stephens and Catherwood saw rows of square stones, meticulously carved and ordered, emerge from the tangle of roots and leaves. They found steps, the corner of a building and the sides of a pyramid. All of a sudden, they found themselves in the presence of a stone colossus. Stephens described the encounter with the silent herald of another era and another people in these terms: "It was about fourteen feet high and three feet on each side, sculptured in very bold relief, and on all four of the sides, from the base to the top. The front was the figure of a man curiously and richly dressed, and the face, evidently a portrait, solemn, stern, and well fitted to excite terror. "The back was of a different design, unlike anything we had ever seen

before, and the sides were covered with hieroglyphics". This our guide called an "Idol"; and before it was a large block of stone, which he called an altar. The sight of this unexpected monument put at rest at once and forever, in our minds, all uncertainty with regard to the character of American antiquities... With an interest perhaps stronger that we had ever felt in wandering among the ruins of Egypt, we followed our guide... who conducted us to fourteen monuments of the same character and appearance, some with more elegant designs, and some equal in workmanship to the finest monuments of the Egyptians. Having seen the classical ruins with his own eyes, the judgement of Stephens was immediate: "America, say historians, was peopled by savages; but savages never reared these structures, savages never carved these stones... Architecture, sculpture,

and painting, all the arts which embellish life, had flourished in this overgrown forest; orators, warriors, and statesmen, beauty, ambition, and glory, had lived and passed away, and none knew that such things had been, or could tell of their past existence. Books, the records of knowledge, are silent on this theme".

One of the most important and largest of the Mayan cities, Copán was situated the furthest south, almost peripheral to the rest of the civilisation, but it nevertheless achieved a cultural and artistic importance equalled by few other centres of the time. It stands at nearly 2000 feet above sea level in the middle of the Copán valley, it is now in the

Page 114 – Stela A (731 AD), rear side with glyphic inscription, Copán.

Page 115 – Map of the site of Copán.

F. Catherwood.   J. J. Günther.

territory of Honduras a few miles from the Guatemalan border. The steep hills that surround the site still hide the remains of many structures while the plateau is dotted with small hills that cover the ruins of temples and palaces. What is known as the "Main Group", or the centre of Copán, is the only area that has been properly excavated and stands on the right bank of the river, the changing course of which has eroded much of the western section of the Acropolis. This nucleus is formed by four well-proportioned "squares", surrounded and connected by large terraces and platforms on which palaces and stepped pyramids stand. Copán developed between 450 and 800 AD and then underwent a mysterious decline followed by abandonment. It is famous for its two massive stone stairways lined with hieroglyphic inscriptions and for the magnificence of its stone sculptures. Today the archaeological site stands in a park of trees hundreds of years old. The magic of the place is very strong: the stelae, the buildings, the pyramids and the large ball-court are all extraordinary evidence of a civilisation which is still largely unknown to us. The ruins of the city's past greatness first appear in the distance as the visitor passes along a narrow path through the thick undergrowth; then, as the path opens, they emerge in all their splendour. As one tours the squares, walks around the ancient buildings or admires the fantastic animal sculptures, the harmony of the carvings with their setting becomes clear, particularly when appreciated with the sound of water and the presence of the enormous trees. The site is imbued with an inexpressible atmosphere that is mixed with the beauty of the Mayan art,

represented by the imposing and richly decorated stelae.

Copán has now become an international tourist destination but it is quite different to what met the eyes of the two explorers. "The city was desolate. No remnant of this race hangs round the ruins, with traditions handed down from father to son, and

Page 116 – Stela I (692 AD), front side, Copán.

Page 117 – Stela N (764 AD), front side, Copán.

from generation to generation. It lay before us like a shattered bark in the midst of the ocean, her masts gone, her name effaced, her crew perished, and none to tell whence she came... The place where we sat, was it a citadel from which an unknown people had sounded the trumpet of war? or a temple for the worship of the God of peace? or did the inhabitants worship the idols made with their own hands, and offer sacrifices on the stones before them? all was mistery, dark, impenetrable mistery, and every circumstance increased it. In Egypt, the colossal skeletons of gigantic temples stand in the unwatered sands in all the nakedness of desolation; here an immense forest shrouded the ruins, hiding them from sight, heightening the impression and moral effect, and giving an intensity and almost a wildness to the interest".

Once they returned to Don Gregorio's hacienda, Stephens and Catherwood started to make plans for the following days but first they wanted to find somewhere else to stay, as far away as possible from their reluctant host. The other inhabitants had begun to take to the visitors, especially as a result of Frederick's powers as a "healer" who had won deserved respect by handing out medicines and liniments to the needy. This respect was increased by the strange practices of the two who astonished their public by cleaning their teeth regularly, "an operation which, probably, they saw then for the first time". Things, however, took

Page 118 – Stela F (721 AD), front side, Copán.

Page 119 – Stela F, rear side with glyphic inscription, Copán.

another turn for the worse when an acquaintance of Don Gregorio, a modest and tidy man, made himself known and claimed to be the only owner of the ruins of Copán. His name was Don José Maria Asebedo. He was one of the most respectable people in the area, about fifty years of age, unusually tall and stubborn. Incited by the Mephistophelean Don Gregorio, he had no intention of yielding to the requests of Stephens

who wanted to camp in the ruins, free them of the vegetation and let Catherwood carry out his valuable surveys and drawings. It was Frederick once again that found a solution to the problem having taken charge of the ailments of Don José's wife in the meantime. Stephens had carefully studied the property documents given to him by Don José and had decided to purchase the entire Mayan city, remove the stelae and other transportable monuments, load them onto rafts, float them down the river as far as the Bay of Honduras, and then ship them from there to New York where he wanted to open the first museum of American archaeology. Luckily for us and for Copán — one thinks of sites like Pergamum, Miletus and other cities in Asia Minor that were stripped of their greatest monuments in the 19th century — the project was unworkable due to rapids in the river. Stephens still wished to buy the site however and remove at least one of the "idols", letting Catherwood make plaster casts of

those remaining. He could already see his name in the history books and hear distinctly the thanks of the New York mayor! In reality, the undertaking was rather laborious and Don Gregorio gave the poor Don José no peace though his mouth was watering at the prospect of the American's money. In the end, as the diplomatic documents with the makeshift US seal had not achieved any result, Stephens remembered his uniform and decided to dress up to make an impression. "I opened my trunk and put on a diplomatic coat, with a profusion of large eagle buttons. I had on a Panama hat, soaked with rain and spotted with mud, a check shirt, white pantaloons, yellow up to the knees with mud... but Don José Maria could not withstand the buttons of my coat". The incredible scene took place on 17 November 1839 when the New York lawyer John Lloyd Stephens bought Copán for fifty dollars. The first methodical research on a Mayan site was begun on that day.

This episode, together with the tale told by Schliemann regarding the discovery of the "treasure of Troy", is one of the most celebrated in the annals of heroic archaeology but it appears today that it should in part be reassessed. In his Incidents of Travel in Central America, Stephens says he bought Copán for the sum cited ("I paid fifty dollars"), but recently the original contract was found on which not his signature is shown but Catherwood's. Moreover, the document states that Don José agreed to lease the land for three years so that "Mr Minister of North America, citizen John L. Stephens" could make his plastercasts of the "sculpted rocks" they found on the site. It is repeated several times that the site was let "only so that drawings of the above-mentioned stones could be made". If Stephens had really believed he had become the owner of Copán and its stelae, he was completely mistaken.

Whatever the truth of the matter, Catherwood finally was free to begin his work. Stephens had also engaged several Indians to help clear the ruins of the vegetation so that the Englishman could take measurements with his theodolite. The first result of these complicated operations performed in trying conditions was the map of Copán which still amazes with its precision; the precision is all the more remarkable if one thinks that the buildings were still little more than ruins despite having been liberated in part from the grip of the wild fig trees. Clearly the abstractionist ability of "Mr Catherwood" was quite extraordinary. He was able to "see" the original appearance of the monuments that had been laboriously returned to the light. Although they were new to him, it was almost easy for him to interpret the architectural

Page 120 – Stela A (731 AD), front side, Copán.

Page 121 – Stela A, right side, Copán.

models of the strange city. It was much more difficult to understand, even with the help of his light chamber, the rules that underpinned Mayan art. Complex friezes, shapes without apparent meaning, ornamental motifs with their inextricable appearance firmly resisted his every attempt to copy them. Stephens described with these words the disappointing encounter between Frederick and one of the Copán stelae: "He was standing with his feet in the mud, and was drawing with his gloves on, to protect his hands from the moschetoes. As we feared, the designs were so intricate and complicated, the subjects so entirely new and unintelligible, that he had great difficulty in drawing. He had made several attempts, both with the camera lucida and without, but failed to satisfy himself or even me, who was less severe in criticism. The idol seemed to defy his art; two monkeys on a tree on one side appeared to be laughing at him, and I felt discouraged and despondent". Fortunately, the downheartedness at first felt by poor Stephens was soon

F. Catherwood   H. Jordan

Page 122 top – Stela N (764 AD), front face: it represents "Rising Sun", the last king of Copán.

Page 122 bottom – Stela D (736 AD), front side, Copán.

Page 123 – Stela D, rear side with glyphic inscription, Copán.

revealed to be without foundation; Catherwood's illustrations are so elegant and detailed that they are used by scholars of the Mayan civilisations to this day.

To be able to explore the whole of Copán, it would have been necessary to cut down all the trees and burn all the undergrowth, but this would have taken an excessive amount of time and the weather was too rainy. Stephens and Catherwood decided to clear each idol and the figurative elements of the various buildings one at a time. Once freed of the clinging vegetation, Frederick could draw them at ease. Each day he became more accustomed to the strange art and began to understand its underlying compositional rules. He worked

ceaselessly and in the meantime Stephens would continue in the clearance of the next monument with the help of several local men.

Catherwood was evermore fascinated by what they discovered each day. As he wrote some years later in the introduction to his Views of Ancient Monuments in Central America, the architectural and sculptural remains freed from the forest showed "a high degree of constructive skill, and attesting, in their ornaments and proportions, to the prevalence of an indigenous and well established system of design, varying from any known models in the old world". Frederick also realised that the Indians they worked with were the direct descendants of the builders of ancient

Copán and the other cities lost in the jungle, the people that had populated the jungle for a period much earlier than the arrival of the first Spanish conquistadors. Unfortunately, three hundred years of foreign domination had reduced the proud Maya "to the condition of agricultural labourers, mostly attached to the great estates by a species of feudal tenure... Unfortunately for the antiquarian they are totally without historic traditions, nor is their curiosity excited by the presence of the monuments amongst which they live, to more than an indistinct feeling of religious romance and superstitious dread".

Although he had no documentary proof, Catherwood soon formed a personal opinion that Maya architecture was essentially religious in nature. And in this too he was right. The gigantic terraced pyramids, so different to Egyptian pyramids,

were not crowned by a point but by large terraces that supported heavy stone structures "unquestionably... erected for purposes of a sacred character". He had also intuited the cruel nature of the rites officiated by the Maya from the shapes of the altars. The offer of human blood was the supreme gift of the Maya to their gods; although the function of many of the stones is still debated, it must be admitted that at least some of them were used for sacrifice. Catherwood also realised that the massive Mayan buildings with their emphasis on the horizontal plane were made up of hollowed parallel structural elements able to resist the frequent earthquakes of Central America. He was greatly curious about the techniques used to

build the arches and vaults, just as he was obliged to create definitions for them as more suitable terms did not exist. In fact, the Mayan vault is unique in the history of architecture: it looks as though it is produced by two parallel walls that get progressively thicker as they reach the top until they touch, leaving a space below the same shape as a peasant's hut. Catherwood had understood the

construction methods, their potential and their limits and was certain that the Maya were close to the discovery of the true arch. In this case too, recent finds not yet studied in depth would seem to confirm his intuition.

As the buildings of Copán were without exception reduced to piles of ruins and covered by exuberant foliage, Catherwood ended up paying all his attention to the sculptural

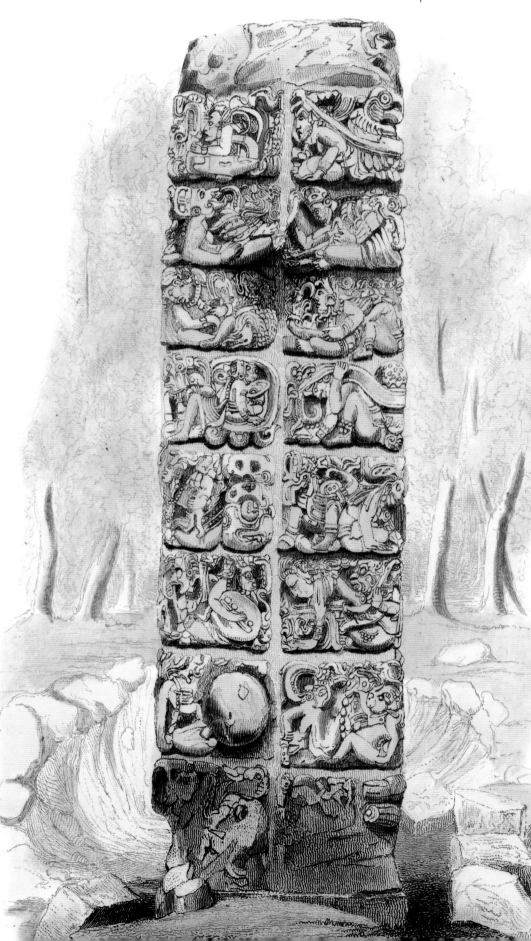

Page 124 centre – Altar Q (776 AD), seen from the northern side with four sovereigns, Copán.

Page 124 bottom – Altar Q, seen from the southern side with four sovereigns, Copán.

Pages 124-125 – Altar Q, seen from the western side with coronation ceremony of the king of the rising sun, Copán.

objects. He portrayed with absolute faithfulness stone fragments, masks, stelae and altars. One of these in particular captured the imagination of the two explorers to the extent that Catherwood drew it from all angles: it is known today as Altar Q and is one of the most exciting objects in Mayan civilisation. Sixteen beautifully dressed figures are sculpted on the sides of a massive, regular six-sided monolith. One of the figures is the Lord Rising Sun who is receiving the insignia of power from one of his forefathers.

The other figures are his predecessors. The surface of the altar is covered with a long hieroglyphic incision showing the date of the coronation, 776 AD.

However much altars and bas-reliefs were worthy of interest, Copán was to all intents and purposes a city of stelae, or "idols" as Catherwood called them. Slim blocks of stone whose "front and back are, in general, representations of human figures, dressed in a most singular manner... The sides are carved with hieroglyphics, which no one has yet

been able to decipher". The problem posed by the inscriptions tormented both explorers, and Stephens, in particular, dreamed of finding a key to their mystery. He couldn't have any idea that more than a century would pass before scholars were able to provide the first, meagre translations. And even today, notwithstanding the enormous strides made during the 1980's and 90's, the Mayan language is still not legible in its entirety and it will require decades to translate the thousands of inscriptions found so far.

IN THE JUNGLE OF CENTRAL AMERICA

The work went on quickly for thirteen days, then Stephens remembered his diplomatic duties. Enthusiastic as he was about their discoveries, his task was to track down the government of Central America, or what was left of it, and now it was time to head on to Nueva Guatemala. Catherwood had made a great number of drawings but not as many as he wanted and was against the idea of leaving. After long consultation, it was decided that Catherwood would remain for a few days more to finish cataloguing and surveying, then he would head for the capital as well.

On 26 November, Stephens started out once more with Augustin into the forest leaving his friend alone, but Catherwood was in good hands as he was now considered a doctor by the local community and he enjoyed a certain prestige as well as the affection of his "patients". At first, the two strangers had been viewed with concern and it was thought they were performing some kind of black magic to find forbidden treasure but after a while even the continual insinuations of Don Gregorio no longer had any effect. The foreigners were rather strange but also authentic gentlemen that did no harm. So Catherwood continued his tiring and patient work, besieged by swarms of mosquitoes and always in fear of scorpions or more dangerous insects.

At the end of an extenuating ride, Stephens entered Nueva Guatemala like a mud statue but happy to have reached his destination as, all in all, he would not risk compromising his political career". The roads were deserted and he only managed to find the house of Mr. Hall, the British vice-consul, with difficulty. Hall quickly outlined the dramatic situation. The soldiers of General Carrera were tired of receiving no pay and rebelled, throwing the city into panic as they turned to robbery and looting. In more general terms, the entire confederation of Central American states was politically dissolved and each member state had now ended in civil war. Travel was

dangerous since bands of guerrillas, disbanded soldiers and common criminals ran riot in villages, killing and terrorizing whoever opposed them. Stephens was disconcerted because the capital had seemed so very beautiful to him, imbued with that romanticism that was peculiar to Spanish cities, with low houses rendered with lime and perfumed plants climbing around the windows. The idyllic appearance was hard to reconcile with the bloody atmosphere that reigned. Once he had taken possession of the building for the American delegation, he decided to follow the diplomatic instructions he had received. He began searching for the Guatemalan government and its representatives, but in vain. Francisco Morazan was in an all-out struggle with Rafael Carrera and the democratic institutions were nothing but a memory. Just then, no-one could have said who represented the political

interests of Guatemala or the whole of Central America. By the end of December, it was clear to Stephens that if ever there had been a semblance of government in Guatemala, it certainly was there no longer. In the meantime, he had met in person the feared and victorious General Carrera who had struck him by his strong personality, but he had been of no help. The only thing Stephens could do was to pack up the documents left in the offices of the embassy and ship them back to the United States. Then, having dispensed with his political duties, he decided to permit himself a little tourism: he visited the ruins of Antigua Guatemala, climbed to the top of the Agua volcano, reached the Pacific coast and passed through a myriad of villages. He indulged his curiosity everywhere he went and he spent most of his time up till Christmas walking in the mountains or wandering

through local market places.

Meanwhile, camped in the ruins of Copán, Catherwood was fighting two personal battles: one to master the redundant and complex art of the Maya in full, the other to defend himself from the mosquitoes. He won the first battle but lost the second. After three weeks spent in the forest, he succumbed to the malaria meted out by the anopheles mosquito. Laid prostrate by the fever, he was also robbed of food, blankets and other materials by one of the mule-drivers. In his suffering, he was forced to knock at the door of Don Gregorio who, to his enormous surprise, welcomed him in and attempted to alleviate the fever (evidently, it was the American who roused the anger of the grumpy old man). As soon as he got better, Frederick wrote to Stephens to explain the situation and decided to follow on in the shortest time possible.

Page 126 – A hut in the midst of a clearing planted with tobacco and maize, Copán. Stephens and Catherwood lived in a similar structure.

Pages 126-127 – The main square of Antigua Guatemala.

During his trip, while he was still on the Motagua river, he learned of another group of ruins hidden in the forest about 28 miles north of Copán and, although he was still weak, he could not resist the temptation to visit them. So it was that he discovered the remains of Quiriguá, today famous for the enormous stelae sculpted out of monuments show the capture of the ruler of Copán, Rabbit 18 (this is how the hieroglyphics that tell us his name are read in the absence of a better interpretation), in 737 during the reign of the 14th king of Quiriguá. Regardless of their political vicissitudes, the local architecture and art are clearly dependent on those of

red sandstone, the largest so far found on Mayan territory.

The city was probably founded around 450 and abandoned shortly after 810. It is similar to Copán in its layout. The ruins of the main group stand around a great rectangular square dotted with stelae and running north-south. The Acropolis stands on the southern side. It was thought that Quiriguá was a colony of Copán for a long time but in 1978 this hypothesis was finally disproved. It seems instead that the two centres were reciprocally hostile: many local nearby Copán and Catherwood immediately understood that. The only difference was that the reliefs on the stelae appeared less accentuated besides being less dynamic in their designs.

Unfortunately, Quiriguá stands in the middle of a wet tropical forest and its more hostile climate than that of Copán meant that Frederick had to follow a fast-flowing river and then cut through a mile of jungle with his machete to reach the site, a task "such as none can fully understand who have not been in a

tropical country". This obviously was not the place for someone recovering from malaria and Frederick only spent enough time there to draw the two best preserved stelae, now identified as E and F.

On Christmas Day, a worn out, pale, thin and armed to the teeth "Mr Catherwood" finally made his entrance to Nueva Guatemala. Stephens welcomed him with great relief, especially as he was preparing to leave on his research. They celebrated New Year and then Stephens wanted to restart his political mission: if there was no government in Guatemala, then he had to look for one in Salvador or one of the other neighbouring countries, but this journey too turned into a nightmare as Stephens also fell prey to malaria. Luckily, Catherwood was with him which was a bonus even if only because the Englishman had had some experience of the subject. "Not having killed any one at Copán, he had conceived a great opinion of his medical skill" and it was Frederick who administered the doses of quinine, making sure they hit the mark. In addition to everything else, Frederick was a precise and well-organised man so that for a few days he saw to the food and all other

practical contingencies. Once they reached the Pacific coast, Stephens went on by boat towards Salvador while Catherwood returned to Copán where he thought he had left too much work unfinished. Once more Don Gregorio, transformed from a gruff and cantankerous old codger into a gentleman, offered him warm hospitality and the Englishman was able to return to his pencils.

While the one continued his archaeological exploration, the other crossed the length and breadth of Salvador, Costa Rica and Nicaragua, passing from one theatre of war to another. After countless vicissitudes, innumerable miles through the forests, strong doses of quinine to hold off recurrent fever, spectacular volcanic landscapes, picturesque villages, gold mines and coffee plantations, Stephens was finally able to return to Nueva Guatemala, richer in experience but having seen neither hide nor hair of a government.

It was the end of March 1840 and at that point the "Mr. Minister of the United States" decided that it was the moment to tender his resignation and hurry off to the ruins of Palenque in the Mexican state of Chiapas as the rainy season would soon begin.

Page 128 top – The expedition progresses with difficulty through the forest. Stephens, exhausted, is carried on the back of a bearer.

Page 128 – Fragment of sculpture, acropolis area, Copán.

Page 129 – Colossal stela, Quiriguá.

Carrera had by now finally defeated Morazan and just installed himself in Guatemala City but he could not by any means be considered a reliable politician. So Stephens wrote a letter to Washington explaining the situation and stating that, given the circumstances, he considered further stay in the country completely unjustified. Finally, Catherwood (after spending a month in a monastery in Antigua to get his health back) knocked once again at the door of the American delegation one evening and the two embraced promising solemnly not to separate again while in such a dangerous place. In early April, the new expedition was ready but before leaving Stephens presented himself to General Carrera to ask for a pass to enable them safe conduct during the difficult journey to Palenque. This Carrera provided with ostentatious pride. The march was of course similar, if not more difficult, than that from Belize to Copán with the jungle throwing up all the obstacles it had at its disposal – mud, rain, creepers, roots, insects and poisonous plants besides the occasional earth tremor. The path grew more laborious as they neared the agave covered highlands of Guatemala and the hostile forests of Petén. The two found the time to stop briefly to explore the remains of Utatlán near Santa Cruz del Quiché, and another Mayan site named Toniná near to Ocosingo in Guatemala, but the two sites were so ruined that Catherwood had little to draw. Near Santa Cruz, the two bumped into a very strange person who turned out to be the priest of the village. He was a cultivated man from Spain who looked upon the world with ferocious irony and knew many

130

A. Palace & Place of Sacrifice
B. Fortress.
C.C.C.C. Barincs which sur-
            rounded the Palace
        on all sides.
D.D.D.D. Small stream.

Page 131 centre – View of the ruins of Utatlán.

Page 131 bottom – View and plan of a pyramid-shaped religious building, Utatlán.

stories about the ancient Maya. Among other things, he told them of a mysterious city that was still populated by descendants of the powerful lords who had built it centuries before. It had white "towers" that poked out over the tops of green trees and was located just four days march away. Although Stephens and Catherwood were tempted, they decided that the time they had available was too limited and with heavy hearts they soldiered on. If instead they had followed the direction of the unusual Dominican priest, they would have found the remains of Tikál, one of the largest and most spectacular Maya cities.

After stopping at Quetzaltenango, a charming city that pleased the artistic tastes of Catherwood, they reached Huehuetenango near the border with Mexico where they were shown several ancient ruins. Here they met an American, John Pawling, who had already met Stephens some weeks before at Amatitlán. Tired of the war engulfing Guatemala, Pawling asked to join their expedition, an "honour" that was quickly accorded him. The last days of the journey were spent in a jungle lashed by rain and divided by fast running rivers and gorges hundreds of feet deep. It was a torment.

Pages 130-131 – Map of the ruins of Santa Cruz del Quiché, the ancient Maya site of Utatlán.

Page 130 bottom – View of a pyramid-shaped religious building in Utatlán.

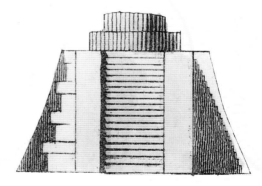

PALENQUE

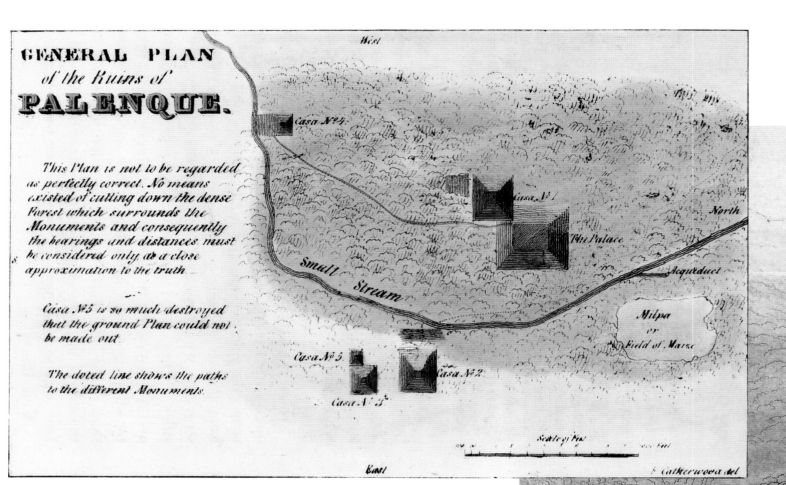

The village of Santo Domingo del Palenque was at last reached on 11 May ; they had taken five weeks to walk the three hundred and ten miles from Nueva Guatemala. At Santo Domingo they learnt of the expedition of Walker and Caddy that had preceded them and that was now on its return. The day following their arrival, the two made their entrance to the silent ruins of the Mayan city.

The ruins of Palenque lie in the valley of the Usumacinta río. It is one of the best known Mayan archaeological sites although it is for the most part unexplored. The entire monumental complex covers an area of 6 square miles and only the centre, the "Main Group", has been cleared of the embrace of the tropical forest. Compared to other Mayan cities, Palenque was "discovered" some time

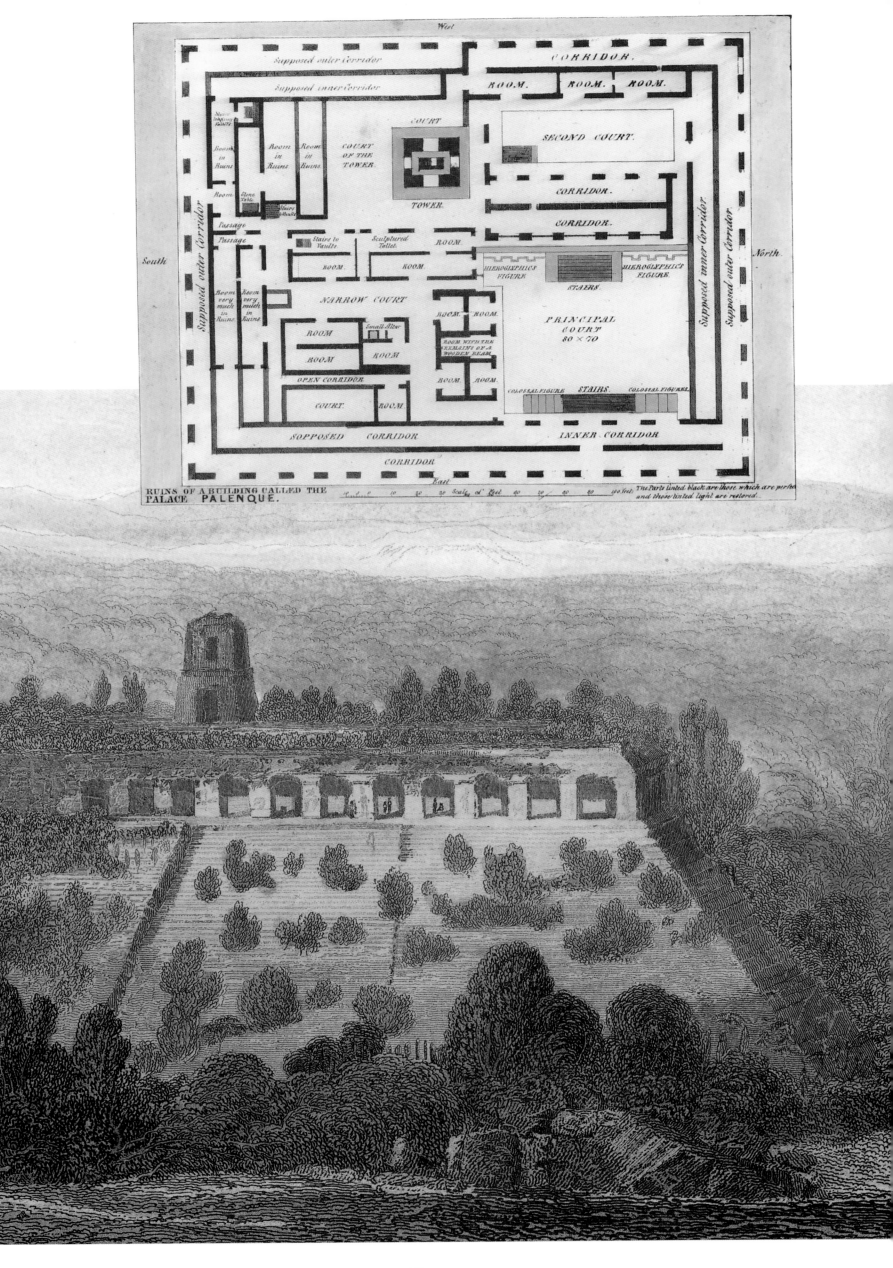

West

Supposed outer Corridor   CORRIDOR.

Supposed inner Corridor   ROOM.   ROOM.   ROOM.

COURT

SECOND COURT.

Room in Ruins

Room in Ruins Room in Ruins COURT OF THE TOWER.

TOWER.

CORRIDOR.

CORRIDOR.

Room Stone Table.

Passage

Passage

Stairs to Vaults.   Sculptured Tablet.   ROOM.

HIEROGLYPHICS FIGURE   STAIRS.   HIEROGLYPHICS FIGURE

South   North

ROOM.   ROOM.

Supposed inner Corridor.

Supposed outer Corridor

Supposed outer Corridor

Room very much in Ruins. Room very much in Ruins

NARROW COURT

ROOM.   ROOM.

PRINCIPAL COURT 80 × 70

ROOM   Small Altar   ROOM.

ROOM   ROOM

ROOM WITH THE REMAINS OF A WOODEN BEAM

OPEN CORRIDOR

ROOM.   ROOM.

COLOSSAL FIGURE   STAIRS   COLOSSAL FIGURE

COURT.   ROOM.

SUPPOSED   CORRIDOR.   INNER CORRIDOR

CORRIDOR.

East

RUINS OF A BUILDING CALLED THE PALACE PALENQUE.

Scale of Feet   10   20   30   40   50   60   70   80   90   100 feet.

The Parts tinted black are those which are perfect and those tinted light are restored.

ago. Padre Solis, a Spanish priest, was sent by his bishop to a rural centre in Chiapas called Santo Domingo in Palenque in 1746; here the priest soon came across "houses of stone" that no-one knew the existence of. From the moment that word spread of the discovery, a long series of explorations by travellers, adventurers and political authorities began. In 1784, the governor of Chiapas, Don José Estacheria, ordered some on-site examinations to check the extent of the discovery, then sent an Italian architect, Antonio Bernasconi, to make a map of the site and estimate its size. Bernasconi realised that the city had not been destroyed by earthquake or fire but abandoned by its inhabitants and then covered by the jungle. Two years later, in 1786, King Charles III of Spain sent the soldier of fortune Antonio del Rio to carry out a reconnaissance of the mysterious ruins. This expedition is considered the beginning of archaeological investigation into pre-Columbian America. Later, the successor to the Spanish throne, Charles IV, sent an exploratory mission to Palenque headed by Colonel Dupaix and the Mexican Luciano Castañeda. It was their report that excited the imagination and curiosity of Stephens and which prompted his trip.

The principal monuments of the ancient Mayan city are rich with inscriptions and their recent decoding has revealed many of the secrets of the site's past and its protagonists. Research has shown that the site was occupied from the 2nd c. AD but its cultural and architectural peak was reached during the period from 615 to 800 AD. This is when the principal monuments were built and the historical inscriptions listing the names and deeds of the rulers were engraved.

Today, the visitor reaches Palenque

Pages 134-135 – The western side of the main courtyard, inside the Palace of Palenque.

Page 135 – Stucco bas-relief in the Palace of Palenque.

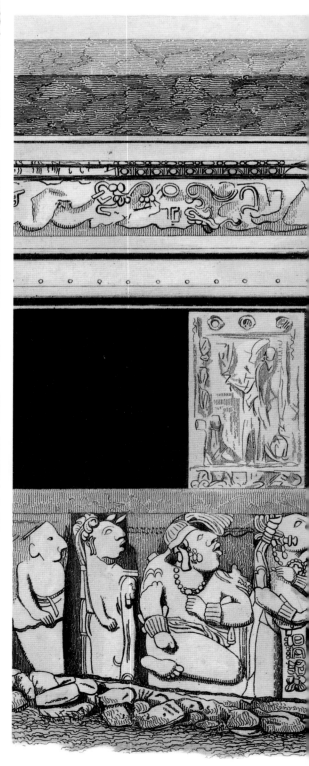

Page 136 – Stucco bas-relief in the western wing of the Palace of Palenque.

Pages 136-137 – The western side of the main courtyard, in the Palace of Palenque.

via a long road that passes the northern area of the city and enters the main square and ceremonial centre. On the eastern side, this vast space is dominated by the monumental complex known as the "Palace". It is thought that the buildings that make it up had a civil function, perhaps as an administrative centre or where audiences were granted by the ruling elite, but these are only hypotheses. The Palace is formed by a tall platform measuring 280 feet long by 200 wide topped by a complex of galleries with porches supported by corbelled vault ceilings and arranged around three large internal courtyards. Traces of the original bas-relief decorations are visible on the square pillars and pitch of the roofs that were originally covered with polychrome stuccoes. Stephens and Catherwood were able to admire the decorations better than we can today given the current state of their preservation. The entire complex is dominated by a four-floor tower that is considered by some to have been a lookout but which is more generally thought to have been an astronomical observatory. The most impressive sacred building at Palenque, the Pyramid of the Inscriptions, stands on the south side of the square. This construction is 120 feet high and made up of nine sections on top of one another. The name is derived from three stone panels inside the top of the temple that are entirely covered with carved hieroglyphs. They form the longest Mayan inscription ever found. In 1952, the archaeologist Alberto Ruiz Lhuillier found a crypt inside the pyramid that contained the sarcophagus of Pacal, the ruler of the

city from 615 to 683, the year of his death.

The ceremonial centre of Palenque also contains other important architectural complexes like the North Group, the Temple of the Count and the ball-court. The "Group of the Cross" was of fundamental importance to the site; it comprised three temples rather smaller than the Pyramid of the Inscriptions – the Temple of the Cross, the Temple of the Foliated Cross and the Temple of the Sun – which were built between 672 and 692 on the orders of the ruler Chan Bahlum, son and successor to Pacal. They stand close to the hill behind the Palace. All three are built in a pyramidal structure with the shrine on the top covered by a mansard roof. This is topped by a complex comb which was once lined with moulded and painted stucco decorations. The names given to the three monuments were suggested by the wall friezes which contain cosmogonic themes of the Mayan world and which were in great part misunderstood by the first discoverers of Palenque.

We will not dwell on the experiences shared by Catherwood and Stephens while they explored the ruins of the ancient city. It is enough to say that, helped by Pawling and

Page 138 – Stucco bas-relief on one of the pillars of the western facade of the Palace of Palenque.

Page 139 – Stucco bas-relief on a door-jamb, in the Palace of Palenque.

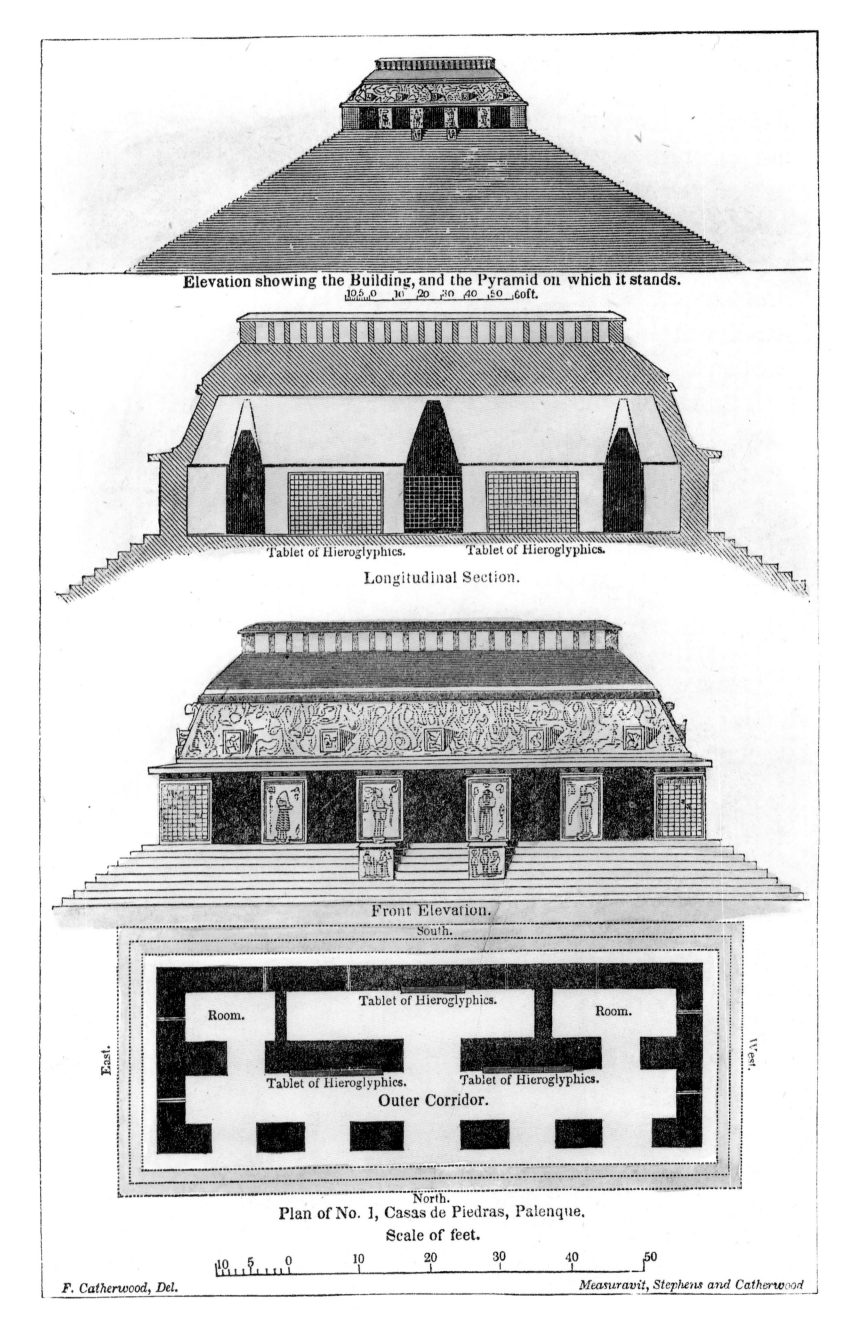

Elevation showing the Building, and the Pyramid on which it stands.

10 5 0   10   20   30   40   50   60 ft.

Tablet of Hieroglyphics.   Tablet of Hieroglyphics.

Longitudinal Section.

Front Elevation.

South.

Room.   Tablet of Hieroglyphics.   Room.

Tablet of Hieroglyphics.   Tablet of Hieroglyphics.

Outer Corridor.

North.

Plan of No. 1, Casas de Piedras, Palenque.

Scale of feet.

10 5 0   10   20   30   40   50

East.   West.

F. Catherwood, Del.   Measuravit, Stephens and Catherwood

Page 140 – Prospects, section and plan of House no. 1, known as the Pyramid of Inscriptions, Palenque.

Page 141 above – Prospects and plan of House no. 2, known as the Temple of the Cross.

Page 141 below – Stone bas-relief on the wall of a room in the Palace of Palenque, showing King Pacal receiving the royal crown from his mother.

Front Elevation.

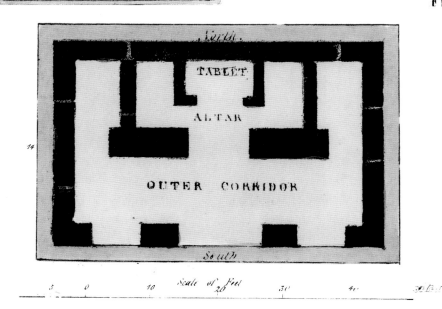

days, Stephens had a swollen foot which was to be further inflamed by insects which entered the skin during the night and laid their eggs. Catherwood was not in any better condition with his left arm blocked by rheumatism, his face and arms all covered by insect bites and his mood black. Not even the visit of some priests from the town of Tumbala lifted their spirits. By now they were close to giving in: after having explored

Indian assistants that had accompanied them from Nueva Guatemala, they measured the entire site and created a reliable ground plan, then freed the more interesting buildings of the jungle plants. Catherwood made dozens of drawings with the aid of his trusty light chamber, noting that here the art appeared more sober than at Copán. The three camped in rooms in the palace where they had arranged all their equipment, food and drawing materials. The mules and a cow they had brought for constant supplies of fresh milk grazed in one of the courtyards. The nights were illuminated by the flickering of myriads of enormous fire-flies and enlivened by the swoops of bats. They slept little, did not eat well enough and the work was exhausting. After a few

141

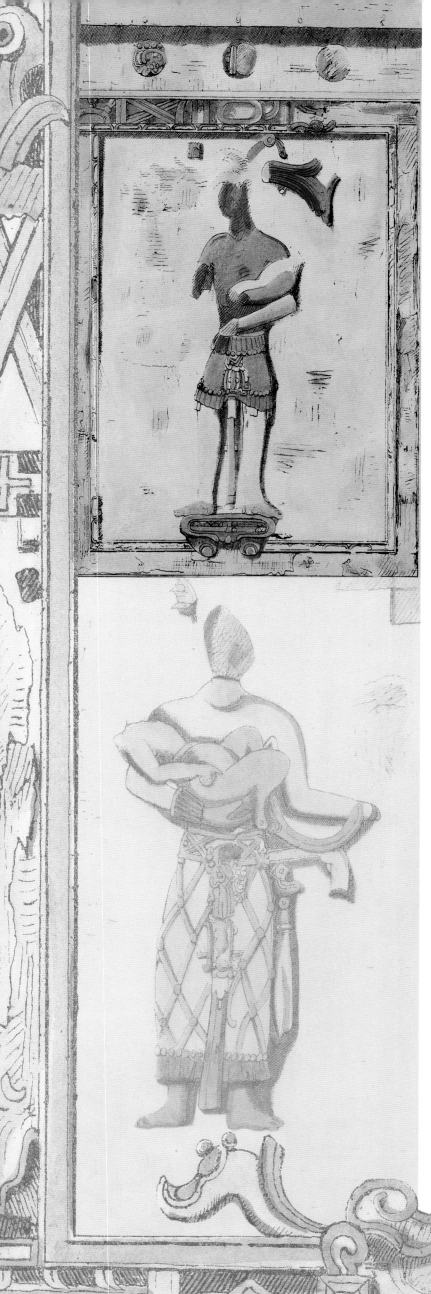

Pages 142 and 143 — Stucco bas-reliefs decorating the four pillars of the facade of the summit temple on the Pyramid of Inscriptions. In three of these, King Pacal is shown holding the God K as a child in his arms; in Maya representations this divinity is always associated with the royal power.

F. Catherwood del.

143

and surveyed the main temples of
Palenque (which they identified with
the Spanish word "casa" followed by
a number), it was clear they could
remain no longer. One day
Catherwood, who was drawing a
splendid polychrome stucco panel,
fainted clean away. Before leaving,
though, Stephens had also got it into
his head to buy Palenque. The price
proposed – 1,500 dollars – was much
more than he had agreed for Copán
but still acceptable. The only problem
was that under Mexican law any
foreigner wanting to buy land had to
marry a local woman, but a couple of
girls from Santo Domingo di
Palenque were really pretty as well as

being interested. It is a pity that the
vigorous, thirty four year old
Stephens, adored by the women,
wanted to remain an impenitent
bachelor – meaning that the purchase
of Palenque came to nothing.

    After spending nineteen days in the
city ruins in unbearable conditions,
besieged by mosquitoes and flies,
lacking sleep from the continuous noise
of the howler monkeys and cicadas,
befuddled by the sultriness of the air
and weakened by a poor diet, the two
succumbed in the end to the violence of
the rainy season. The wall of water
that crashed down pitilessly on the
surrounding forest produced a ceaseless
drumming sound that forced them to
capitulate. "Everything susceptible of
injury from damp was rusty or
mouldy, and in a ruinous condition;
we ourselves were not much better".

Pages 144-145 – Stucco panel in relief
on the rear wall of the sanctuary, in the
Temple of the Sun, Palenque.

On the fourth of June, they left Palenque forever, "like rats that abandon the ship after the shipwreck", and headed for Mérida, the largest town in the Yucatán. As was to be expected, the march was as uncomfortable as possible, winding for days through swamps, savannah infested with insects and verdant lagoons. While crouching in a canoe on the waters of Catazaja in the middle of a profusion of variously coloured birds of all species, Stephens realised and regretted that he was totally ignorant of the natural sciences. Catherwood was ill and when they finally arrived at the port of Laguna de Carmen on the gulf of Mexico after a dreadful crossing of the Terminos lagoon, Stephens was greatly relieved. But "Mr Catherwood" was not the type to declare himself beaten easily. He knew that Stephens was desperate to discover other lost cities and he declared himself ready to continue.

F. Catherwood   A.L. Dick.

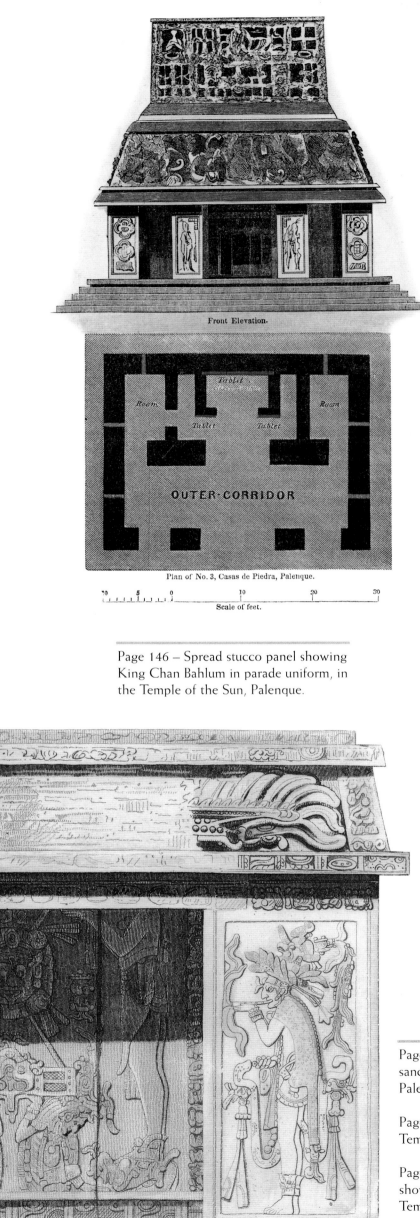

Front Elevation.

Tablet
Room *Tablet* *Room*
Tablet *Tablet*

OUTER-CORRIDOR

Plan of No. 3, Casas de Piedra, Palenque.

Scale of feet.

Page 146 – Spread stucco panel showing King Chan Bahlum in parade uniform, in the Temple of the Sun, Palenque.

F. Catherwood

A.L. Dick.

Pages 146-147 – Prospect of the sanctuary inside the Temple of the Sun, Palenque.

Page 147 left – Prospect and plan of the Temple of the Sun, Palenque.

Page 147 right – Spread stucco panel showing the infernal God L, in the Temple of the Sun, Palenque.

From Carmen (where they left Pawling) they sailed as far as Sisal, the port of the lovely and large colonial city of Mérida, where they arrived on a broken down cart on the eve of Corpus Domini. Here Frederick literally collapsed devoured by malaria.

While in New York, Stephens had met a Hispano-American gentleman

UXMAL

Page 148 – A detail of the facade of the Governor's Palace, Uxmal.

Pages 148-149 – View of the ruins of Uxmal. To the right, the so-called "Pyramid of the Diviner", to the left the Quadrilateral of the Nuns.

by the name of Simón Peón who was a direct descendant of the Montejos, the true owners of the Yucatán from the 17th century on. He had invited Stephens to visit if he was passing through Mérida, adding that he was the owner of an entire ancient city, Uxmal, that would be of great interest. Stephens immediately went to find the principal residence of the Peón family but, unfortunately, Don Simón was at his hacienda in Uxmal about fifty miles off at the time. The two set off straightaway despite Catherwood's fever. Once they arrived at the hacienda, as Frederick was too weak to continue, the American left him in the care of their generous hosts and went off alone to visit the ghost city. He was met by a wonderful surprise because Uxmal, far from being suffocated by the exuberant tropical

forest, stood superb on a plateau dotted only with bushes. The gigantic buildings were in an excellent state of preservation and so richly detailed as to leave Stephens quite breathless. Stephens hurried back to Catherwood to describe what he had seen and the invaluable Englishman had the courage to get back on his feet the next day, collect his drawing materials and mount his mule. It was

all true and even better than he had expected. He began to work furiously with his light chamber and tripod, made several drawings and then collapsed under the blazing sun. Stephens, frightened to death, understood that it was time to go home and that the expedition had to come to an end. They had explored and portrayed in detail three large Mayan cities plus other smaller ones and had

to be content with that. On 24 June, they boarded a Spanish brig headed for Cuba where they were annoyingly held up for several days by a dead calm. This time it was Stephens who was the nurse as Catherwood was really exhausted. Luckily for them, when the drinking water was almost completely finished, together with all hope, an English ship was sighted heading north that took them on board.

HOME AGAIN

On 31 July 1840, almost ten months since their departure, Stephens and Catherwood returned to New York. Once Frederick regained his strength and health under the care of his wife, he began the massive amount of work necessary to prepare the illustrations for Stephens' new book. The publishing company, Harper Bros., intended to ride on the back of the success of the adventurous lawyer's two previous travel diaries and so gave Stephens carte blanche. Their only pressing request was that he go to work as soon as possible since the outcome of the expedition had already been widely published by the American press and the Harper brothers did not want some unexpected explorer to beat them to the finish line. Stephens got permission to have the book published in two large format books, got Harper Bros. to promise that the price to the public would be reasonable so as not to preclude a large number of sales and, most important, ensured that all the artwork, including the cover drawings, were to be entrusted to Frederick. First of all, Catherwood sent some of the finished drawings to London for the xylographic matrices to be treated because the English engravers were reputed to be the best in the world; the results, however, did not satisfy either of them. As they did not have the time to go to London to oversee the work, it was decided that the drawings would have to be incised on steel by five of the best New York professionals. Frederick watched the test prints of every one of the seventy seven illustrations, making alterations where necessary. Considering the hurry with which the artist and engravers had to work, the result was truly impressive. The quality was so good that the copies of the hieroglyphic inscriptions – at the time completely incomprehensible – can today easily be deciphered by experts. This is a testament to the prodigious skill of Catherwood's calligraphic precision. We can deduce from a letter sent in January 1841 to the celebrated writer William Prescott that Stephens had practically finished drafting his lengthy manuscript, but he delayed delivery to Harper Bros. by a few months as he was attempting to conclude an old plan he had begun while in Nueva Guatemala: that of purchasing some of the Maya stelae and transferring them to New York. After his first failure while in Copán, he had now turned his attention to Quiriguá though he had only been able to admire the drawings made by Frederick. He contacted the owners of the site, the Payes brothers, and laboriously attempted to negotiate a deal with the minimum of publicity. If he had published his book immediately and it had met with the success he expected, the reviews might have appeared in the Nueva Guatemala newspapers and so focus too much attention on the local antiquities. Even worse, the prices would inevitably have risen with unpleasant speed. Stephens intended to purchase fourteen items, load them onto rafts, float them down the Motagua river and then ship them to New York where he would then have the nucleus of his longed-for Museum of American Antiquities. Once again though, things did not go right. The Payes brothers were told (by the improvident intervention of the French consul in Guatemala) of the enormous sums of money required to remove certain Egyptian monuments; this the consul knew from the transfer of an Egyptian obelisk from Luxor to Paris in 1836. Convinced that Stephens was backed by his government, the Payes brothers raised their price well beyond the reach of the American to twenty thousand dollars. This was far too high just for the purchase of the monuments even for an author of best-sellers! Downhearted, Stephens delivered the manuscript and Catherwood's illustrations to Harper's in May. Finally, at the end of June, Incidents of Travel in Central America, Chiapas, and Yucatan appeared in the bookshops and, once again, the public was enthusiastic in its response. The book had to be reprinted eleven times in six months although the cover price – five dollars – was not pocket money. By December, the book had sold twenty thousand copies and had become the greatest success of the American publishing trade. Even the critics were flattering and many wrote that Stephens was the most gifted popular writer the United States had ever had. Once again Edgar Allan Poe did not stint in his praise and many observed that a great part of the attraction of the book lay in its splendid and detailed illustrations. Unlike Count Waldeck and all his predecessors, Catherwood had been the only one to portray the essence of Mayan art and architecture and to have reproduced it objectively so confirming its absolute originality. He had been able to see what no-one had previously wanted to believe possible. For the first time, with the help of Stephens' brilliant descriptions and from Catherwood's accurate drawings, the unquestionable truth emerged: that the Mesoamerican civilisations had been indigenous and completely unrelated to any culture that had not been American. An entire castle of absurd theories founded on senseless speculations was destined to collapse. Stephens and Catherwood had built the foundation of modern pre-Columbian archaeology and created the presuppositions on which future scholars were to base their work. It had not been the Israelites, the Egyptians, the Phoenicians, the Romans or the Khmer to found Copán, Palenque, Quiriguá, Uxmal or the other cities hidden in the jungle, but the Maya, a people that had spread their cultural and artistic dominion over a vast area and in a less remote era than the "erudite" scholars had obstinately upheld for decades. Of course the book received criticism, even poisonous criticism, from advocates of the old theories that was as obtuse as it was inconsistent. What counted though was that the two explorers had given future generations a heritage of incalculable value. Some realised this

immediately: those who were not afraid of viewing new horizons recognised the value of what had been shown them and applauded the work and the courage of the two authors without reserve. The public was attracted more than anything else by the suggestive prose of Stephens and by Catherwood's exotic views, but scholars and men of culture like William Prescott knew that the indignant objections raised by the academic world would soon fall into oblivion.

Catherwood and Stephens were beginning to enjoy their deserved success when their plans were upset by the sterile polemic initiated by the young Austrian baron, Emmanuel von Friedrichstal. He had met Stephens on his return from Central America and had decided to visit the Yucatán himself in search of new ruins. Equipped with a daguerreotype machine, he reached the site of Chichén Itzá where he took the first historically ascertained photographs of an American archaeological site (a certain number were exhibited in New York, Paris and London but all trace of them has been lost). When he returned to Europe he was welcomed triumphantly, but in August 1841 an article appeared in the most important newspapers accusing Catherwood of having made drawings that were inaccurate and misleading. Frederick did not take this well at all and printed an open letter in a New York newspaper in which he stated that Friedrichstal "had not set foot" in Copán, Quiriguá, Palenque or any other site described in the book except Uxmal. It was here that Catherwood had stopped only for two days and been able to complete only three drawings, one of which was the plan of the city. As the Baron had no daguerreotype of the two remaining drawings, it could be deduced that no comparison could be made between the pictures made by the two explorers and that therefore the accusations had no basis.

This apart, "Mr Catherwood" had no reason to complain. Business was going great guns, thanks to the sensible management of the Panorama by George Jackson, and his name was by now well-known. His family was now living in a more substantial house and his bouts of malaria were no longer

Pages 150-151 – Stucco panel in relief on the rear wall of the sanctuary inside the Temple of the Cross, Palenque.

tormenting him. Yet Frederick, who had promised himself never to undertake such a risky adventure again, easily agreed to pack his bags and the tools of his trade when Stephens asked him to accompany him on a second trip to Central America. He knew of course that his task had not been finished and that although the jungle had nearly killed him, it still hid its secrets. It was a challenge he could not refuse. Stephens had already pocketed a considerable sum from the sales of his new book (his contract had guaranteed him a net profit of one dollar, ten cents for each copy sold) and so the money to sponsor this trip was not lacking. Further receipts had come from the sales of 2,500 copies of the book in England which was distributed by John Murray. The public wanted another adventure, the publishers wanted another book and Stephens ardently wanted to unveil the secrets of the Yucatán.

Preparations were hurried and the lawyer this time advertised for a third member of the group, a naturalist of proven experience who would make up for Stephens' own lack of biological knowledge. A young surgeon from Boston replied to the advertisement, one Samuel Cabot. With his passion for ornithology, he was the right man for the job, especially as his medical knowledge was to prove itself valuable in such a hostile environment. The party was ready to leave.

THE SECOND EXPEDITION

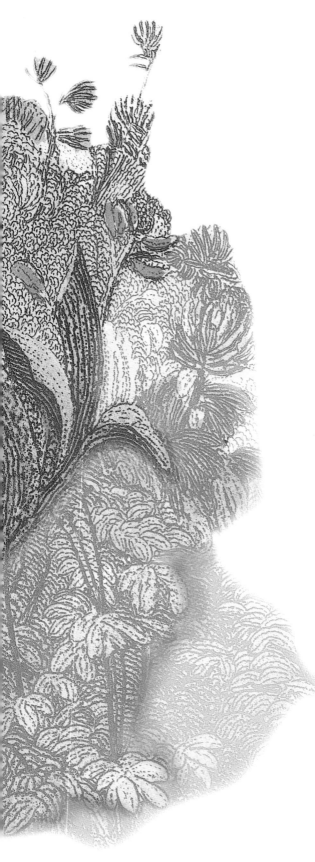

Stephens, Catherwood and Doctor Cabot boarded the Tennessee on 9 October 1841. Their departure took place almost in secret as they did not want to arouse too much curiosity, nor to be followed by annoying "competitors". Their first destination was Sisal where they unloaded all their equipment. Then they headed for the beautiful city of Mérida that had so much attracted Stephens and Catherwood the first time.

The equipment this time included a "daguerreotype apparatus", the forerunner of modern photographic cameras in which the picture was produced on a silver plate. This revolutionary technique had been introduced to the United States in September 1839 by an Englishman, D.W. Seager, who had constructed the first American photographic apparatus by following the instructions in a manual written by the Frenchman, Daguerre. Stephens was acquainted with this technological feat, he also knew Seager and there is proof that Catherwood could have had a similar apparatus during his first trip. The results though were so disastrous as to induce Stephens not to mention them; on the second trip, however, Catherwood practised by first

Pages 152-153 – Map of the Yucatan, with the route followed by Stephens, Catherwood and Cabot.

MAP OF

YUCATAN.

Note. The outline of the Coast is taken from the English and Spanish charts, chiefly from the former, and is supposed to be accurate.
The dotted line ——— points out our route from Sisal, to our return to that Port, and is principally laid down from bearings and distances, and of course only approximates to correctness.
The Latitudes of Mérida and Uxmal, are laid down from meridian altitudes of the Sun.
The Places engraved in outline letters, are taken from manuscript maps, and are probably very far from accurate, no survey of the country having ever been made and published.
A line ——— thus under the name of a Place signifies that there are ruins there.

F. Catherwood

GULF OF

MEXICO

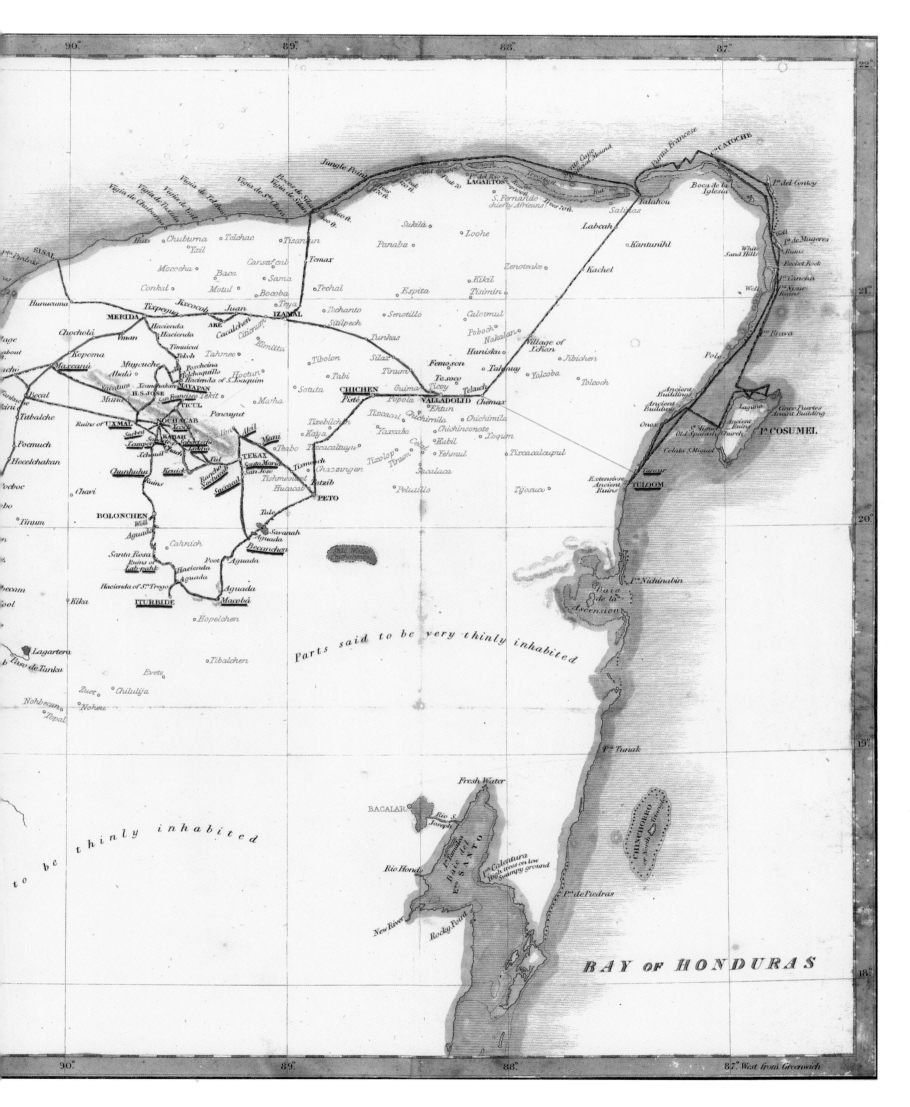

MAYAPÁN

Page 154 left – The mysterious circular building of Mayapán, possibly an astronomical observatory similar to the Caracol of Chichén Itzá.

Page 154 right and page 155 top – Statuettes and fragments of sculpture found in Mayapán.

photographing the pretty girls of Mérida with better results. The machine was later successfully used to portray the Mayan ruins but unfortunately not a single plate has survived to the present day. This would seem to confirm that a malevolent spirit dogged the life's work of our unlucky hero.

As the ups and downs of the first trip to Central America have been discussed at some length, and it is easily inferred that the second

expedition was equally, if not more, adventurous, just a summary of the movements of the three explorers will be given.

Returning to Mérida, the affable Don Peón wanted to introduce Stephens and his companions to the governor of the Yucatán before they set off. His Excellency, Don Santiago Mendez, had read of the celebrated author of Incidents of Travel in Central America and his talented English friend and wanted to meet

them in person. He said he was honoured to welcome them once more to the country and promised them every possible help to ensure their expedition was a success. This was to be hoped for because, for once, Stephens and Catherwood were in a country that was not at war, at least not yet. Exhausted by the diplomatic formalities, the three set off. They were accompanied by the joyous well-wishes of the population of Mérida that had been favourably impressed

by Catherwood's photographic ability and by the surgical skill of Cabot who had operated on dozens of men and women affected by strabismus, widespread among descendants of the Maya.

First they went to the ruins of Mayapán, an important Mayan city that had dominated the Yucatán federation since the 12th century, including Chichén Itzá and Uxmal. Mayapán was finally destroyed in 1441 (or 1460) by Uxmal. Here Catherwood reproduced the ruins of an unusual round building, one of

the few known of in Mayan architecture. Slowly the expedition continued to Uxmal, the city in ruins where they had been forced to interrupt their exploration because of Catherwood's illness before. It seemed as though life itself had abandoned the immense plain - not a river or a stream disturbed the monotony of the desolate karstic expanses covered with scrub - but the unforgettable and unexpected vision of the ruins was enough to give the explorers back their courage. The magnificent buildings of Uxmal were offered up to their eyes in all their splendour.

Around 800 AD, during the Late Classic Period when the Mayan cities had reached a notable economic and political development in the lowlands (where Palenque and Copán stood), a decline set in due to causes that are still unknown. Almost all the cities were suddenly abandoned and all trace of them was lost until the 18th century when the first explorers found them hidden in the depths of the forest.

Page 155 – The great stepped pyramid of Mayapán, known as the "Castillo" and similar to the structure of the building of the same name in Chichén Itzá.

Page 156 top – The southern side of the Governor's Palace, Uxmal.

Pages 156-157 – Sight of Uxmal from the courtyard of the Quadrilateral of the Nuns; on the background, from the left, the Pyramid of the Old Lady, the House of the Turtles, the Governor's Palace, the Grand Pyramid, the Southern Group and the Quadrilateral of the Pigeon-loft.

Page 157 top – Map of the site of Uxmal.

UXMAL

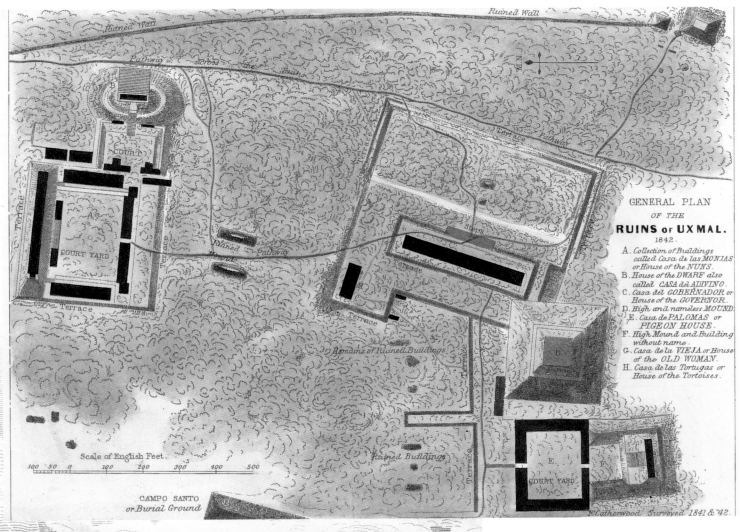

In the Yucatán, however, a different situation arose: between 800 and 900 AD, many small centres that had until then played a marginal role in Mayan affairs underwent an unexpected artistic and architectural expansion which was undoubtedly linked to a remarkable economic progress. The cause of this change of situation was due to the arrival of Maya-Chontál people. They came from the north and were strongly connected with the cultures of the Mexican highlands which had recently reached their cultural peak. It was during this period that the cities of Uxmal, Sayil, Labná, Kabah and others flourished and their remains are to be seen across the Yucatán. Although each centre had its own town-planning characteristics, they shared an architectural style known

CATHERWOOD.

Page 158 left – The inside of the eastern
wing of the Quadrilateral of the Nuns.

Page 158-159 top – One of the stone
masks of the God Chac which adorned
the palaces of Uxmal.

Page 158-159 bottom – The facade of the
eastern wing of the Quadrilateral of the
Nuns, seen from the inner courtyard.

STRONG.SC.

today as "Puuc", from the name of the region where it is mainly found. Elements that distinguish this style are high quality mosaics made from cut stone laid dry on the facades of buildings, the use of the corbelled vault, round columns and the widespread use of masks of the god Chac and the Terrestrial Monster as ornaments.

Of all the Mayan centres in the Yucatán, Uxmal is the most impressive, both for its extraordinary state of preservation and for the size of the site. The most famous monument in the city is the Pyramid of the Magician, also known as the

Pyramid of the Soothsayer, named after a legend that tells of a dwarf magician who won a bet with his king that he could construct the building in a single night. The construction is a gigantic truncated cone on an elliptical base, 85 feet high, that was rebuilt and restructured several times during different epochs. Two steep stairways lead to three temples placed at different heights: the entrance to the one that faces west, just below the shrine on the top, is formed by the wide open jaws of an enormous serpent encircled by grotesque masks of the god Chac. From the top of this amazing building, Catherwood and

Page 160 – Section of the western wing of the Quadrilateral of the Nuns; on the door there are three masks of the God Chac.

Pages 160-161 – Central section of the western wing of the Quadrilateral of the Nuns, with the full figure of a warrior.

Stephens could admire the entire expanse of ruins that was to be their home for six weeks.

Next to the pyramid stood the "Quadrilateral of the Nuns", a large structure given this name by the first Spanish explorers because of its resemblance to a convent. Indeed, the four blocks that compose the structure are arranged around a vast four-sided court and divided into small parallel rooms that, from close up, look like an

example of European monastic architecture. The Quadrilateral of the Pigeon-loft that stands in the shadow of the Great Pyramid is a similar though smaller structure. The name comes from the perforated design of the roof combs that resemble a pigeon-loft.

The most impressive building in the city is found in the south-eastern area; this is the "Palace of the Governor" and it is where the three explorers camped for their entire stay at Uxmal.

The name "Palace of the Governor" was contrived by Brother Lopez de Cogolludo, a Spanish monk that visited the monument and described it in his memoirs published in 1688 as the ancient residence of the rulers of Uxmal. Considered one of the most beautiful buildings in pre-Columbian America, the Palace was built on an enormous platform formed by three terraces with a wide central stairway to reach the top. The four-sided building is 105 yards long by 13 wide and divided into three blocks with two recesses in the centre in which corbelled portal vaults open. Like other buildings at Uxmal, the interior is divided into many small rooms like cells. The mosaic decoration on the upper part of the facade and the austere simplicity of the lower section are typical of Puuc architecture of the Late Classic Period. Although many scholars believe the

UXMAL

UXMAL

Pages 162-163 — Partial view of the so-called "Quadrilateral of the Pigeon-loft", with its tall crests which have given the name to the building.

Page 163 — The facade of the House of the Turtles, which owes its name to the sculptures surmounting the mullioned frieze.

Palace was a real royal court in which audiences and important ceremonies were held, its true function is still unknown despite our knowledge that it was built on a precise astronomical orientation. From the central door, the Mayan astronomers were able to observe the rising of Venus each morning from behind a pyramid some miles away.

Uxmal contains many complexes

Cabot were camped on the site.

Helped by Cabot who was often willingly distracted by the sight of the brightly coloured birds that populated the ruins, Stephens and Catherwood cleaned and measured most of the buildings. The first achievement was an accurate site plan. Then Frederick started to draw the single buildings paying particular attention to the "Governor's Palace". His formidable

and single buildings of extreme interest such as the Great Pyramid, the North Acropolis, the House of the Turtles, the Cemetery Group and the ball-court. Unfortunately, there is no inscription that can throw light on the reigning dynasties or historical events of the city. Little progress has been made in this field since Stephens, Catherwood and

experience told him that the construction techniques were the same as those used at Copán and Palenque although the decorations seemed different. They were therefore studying the remains of a people that at one time had extended its cultural influence over a vast territory. Stephens, meanwhile, had been studying the archives of nearby

UXMAL

villages and had discovered the Spanish transcription of a Mayan chronicle, the "Chilam Balam"; he too began to make connections between the various cities that they had explored up to that moment. All were built from stone on the basis of similar architectural rules and in each they had found inscriptions composed of the same symbols. For the American, the art and historical development of the cities they had visited made the

scholars but it was to be confirmed fifty years later by archaeologist Alberto Ruiz Lhuillier and other excavation programmes in the decades that followed.

Unfortunately, three weeks after their arrival, Stephens fell victim once more to malaria. It sent him into a fever and thoroughly weakened him. The priest of Ticúl, a nearby village where they were later to find more Mayan ruins, took Stephens into the

Mayan civilisation, by then, an incontrovertible reality. Another point of interest was that during his journeys around Uxmal, Stephens had discovered a small Mayan pyramid fallen into rubble in a locality called El Laberinto near Maxcanú. Inside the pyramid he found a passage and he deduced that maybe other pyramids also had hidden rooms inside. This hypothesis was completely ignored by

monastery to take care of him but shortly afterwards both Cabot and an Indian servant, Albino, went down with the same illness. This time round, "Mr Catherwood" seemed to have been passed over and, while the poor priest was coping with three patients, he completed the entire documentation of the ruins of Uxmal alone. In the end though, he too succumbed to malarial fever.

Page 164 – The eastern side of the
Pyramid of the Magician.

Pages 164-165 – The western side of the
same building: the magnificent temple
with entrance with serpent jaws is in the
Chenes style, the top one in the *Puuc*
style.

KABAH

When the three were ready to leave on January 1st 1842, the mules were loaded with chests filled with drawings, maps, original finds (including a carved wooden architrave found in the "Palace of the Governor") and plastercasts of the most representative sculptures and ornaments they had found. Their destination was Kabah, another large city that was once connected to Uxmal by an important road. The road was the means by which most commercial trade in the region had been carried out; a large and austere gateway with a corbelled vault marked its start.

Today this ancient Mayan centre has not been entirely excavated but is known for the Palace of the Masks, or Codz Pop which in the local language means "rolled mat". The entire facade of the building is decorated with large masks of Chac, the god with the long nose, which severely tested Catherwood's skill. To gain access to each room in the palace, it is necessary to climb up a step formed by the upturned nose of a mask which indeed resembles a rolled up mat. The other buildings in the ceremonial centre are

Pages 166-167 – The "Terzera Casa", one of Kabah's monumental buildings.

Page 167 bottom – Map of the site of Kabah.

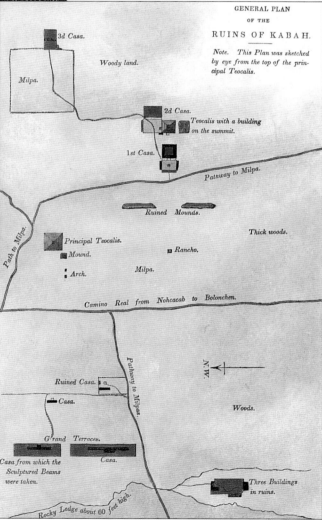

less abundantly decorated but boast lines of innumerable small columns.

Stephens was in seventh heaven because this was the first city he could say he had really "discovered". At that moment, it was still unheard of in the western world. Consequently, no white man had ever been seen in the local villages and stories began to circulate

measurements, drew his usual faultless map of the city and then dedicated his time to drawing the single buildings and ornamental elements. Among these, a splendid architrave made from carved sapodilla wood stands out. It showed a priest or other high dignitary wearing a complex head-dress made of feathers and it was a

about the foreigners searching for dead cities and carrying round mysterious apparatus that smacked of magic. At this point, the diplomatic talent of Albino became indispensable. After problems had been nipped in the bud and the monuments cleared of foliage, Catherwood made his usual

very rare piece. Unfortunately it was inauspiciously destroyed once it reached New York. Other carved stone door jambs were also packed up, sent to Mérida and dispatched to the United States. All trace of them was lost after Stephens' death but they were later found and can now be admired

Page 168 top – The entrance arch to the centre of Kabah, beneath which the old road for Uxmal passed.

Pages 168-169 – The "Secunda Casa", another of the great palaces of Kabah.

Page 169 – A section of the facade of the "Primera Casa", a splendid building known today as Codz Pop, Kabah.

in the American Museum of Natural History in New York. For Stephens, Kabah was the proof of the single architectural style that was common to the Maya throughout Honduras, Guatemala and Mexico. Even the hieroglyphs that adorned the wood panels were the same as those seen previously.

Page 170 – The architrave carved in sapodilla wood, discovered by Catherwood in one of the palaces of Kabah.

Page 171 – Two stone jambs sculpted in bas-relief, found in Kabah, showing a senior dignitary before a kneeling figure.

SABACHSHÉ

Page 172 – Monumental building in
Sabachshé, typical example of
architecture in the Puuc style.

Pages 172-173 – The famous Palace of
Sayil, with widespread use made of
columns with quadrangular capital,
typical of the Puuc style.

Page 173 below – One of the palaces of
Sayil. The small half columns adorning
the facade are known as *junquillos con
ataduras*, or "trunks bound together".

*After leaving Kabah, they headed
south-east and reached the ruins of
Sayil in early February. This site is
home to one of the most extraordinary
Mayan monuments: it is called the
"Palace" and is a large, three storey
construction built on a vast plinth. The
three sections of the building decrease in
depth to create a stepped effect; access to
the top is given by a large central
stairway.*

*From Sayil, the party continued
to Sabachshé where the ruins were
invaded by thick vegetation.
Frederick was increasingly tending to
estrange himself, concentrating as
hard as he possibly could in the
attempt to document all he saw.
Often he worked surrounded by
Indians who watched curiously and
respectfully as he reproduced reality
as if by magic.*

SAYIL

Page 174 – The southern facade of the main building in Labná.

Pages 174-175 – The north western facade of the Arch of Labná; above the two lateral doors there are two friezes representing stylized typical Maya huts.

Page 175 centre – South eastern facade of the so-called "Arch" of Labná, in actual fact a covered passageway between two monumental complexes.

Page 175 bottom – The "Mirador" of Labná, a temple surmounted by a high, elaborate crest complex.

LABNÁ

Then they moved on to Labná, the centre that shows one of the most successful examples of Puuc architecture. Its most interesting monument is a magnificently decorated, large arch realised with the usual method of a corbelled vault. Despite its formal resemblance to a classical triumphal arch, it was in reality a covered passage between two palaces which are today little more than rubble.

The following month, the expedition visited twelve Mayan settlements (many of which are still mostly unexplored) with the difficult task of surveying ruins and the surrounding territory.

Pages 176-177 – The ruins of Xampón.

Page 176 – The main palace of Kiuik: the two panels running alongside the door, decorated with large *junquillos*, are of great interest.

Page 177 top – One of the splendid buildings of Chunhuhu, in Puuc style.

Page 177 bottom – One of the three stone Sacbey buildings: the name derives from the Maya word *sacbé*, "white road".

At Kiuik they came across an unusual limestone slab which was part of a palace frieze painted with the effigy of a sumptuously dressed figure. Stephens had it taken down but it was too heavy to be carried and they had to leave it on the spot. When they were close to Nohcacab, Frederick had a violent attack of fever and fainted in the middle of the road. From that moment on, the health of the party continued to worsen.

While Catherwood and Cabot were lying ill in their hammocks, Stephens found time to visit the village of Ticúl where the patronal festival was taking

XAMPÓN, KIUIK, CHUNHUHU AND SACBEY

place. Here he met an uncommon individual named Juan Pío Pérez, a scholar who had walked many miles to meet Stephens. Pérez gave Stephens one of his books called Antigua Chronologia Yucateca *in which many of the secrets of Mayan astronomy and their calendar were revealed (Stephens later inserted a translation of this work into his own book). Then the two invalids got back on their feet and the group moved off in the direction of Bolonchén where there were famous underwater springs. They passed the ruins of "Sacbey" (actually a Mayan postal station built along one of the extraordinary raised roads called "sachbé" that crossed the region), Xampón, Chunhuhu and other minor sites and eventually reached their objective. The name Bolonchén means "nine wells" and these natural phenomena all*

LABPHAK AND MACOBÁ

appear in the town square. Their cool, clean water was the site's major asset. Having heard of a grotto in the area, the three could not resist visiting it. It was a spectacular chasm created by the action of underground water on the fragile limestone typical of all of the Yucatán. A ramp made of tree-trunks lashed together formed a path

rains, sleepless nights, exhaustion and a lack of food not made up for by roast iguana had enfeebled their spirits and bodies. As if to maintain alive an old tradition to which Catherwood and Stephens were attached against their will, bloody fighting broke out in Yucatán. After centuries of domination, the Indians were rebelling

Page 178 top – The large three-storey palace of Labphak (now Santa Rosa Xtampak), one of the most important examples of the Chenes style.

Page 178 bottom – A stone bas-relief, from the Labphak palace.

Page 179 top – The Macobá ruins.

on the bottom of a passage which led to a vast natural chamber. In here, the real springs had formed pools that, since time immemorial, guaranteed drinking water to the inhabitants of the area.

Next it was the turn of the ruins of Labphak (now known as Santa Rosa Xtampak) where eight stelae decorated with historical scenes rise and rests of a large three-storey palace stand in the middle. Here Catherwood suffered another bout of fever. The continuous

against their white estate owners. Frederick's health worsened daily until he was just a shadow of himself, and similarly his mood worsened. Dehydrated by fever and dysentery, he could no longer stand direct sunlight and was forced to work under a makeshift parasol. Once they arrived at the ruins of Iturbide (the ancient Dzibilnocac), Stephens proposed to interrupt the expedition because he too was physically suffering. "Mr. Catherwood", always so self-

controlled, opposed him firmly. Over the following days there was more friction between Catherwood and Cabot which put Stephens' patience to the test. Then forced company of such different characters was resulting in friction. Anyway, the three, accompanied as always by Albino, managed to reach Chichén Itzá following the ancient raised Mayan road for long distances. During the trip they had come across the remains of Macoba, Yakatzib and other Mayan centres. Stephens had never missed an opportunity to visit local archives on their way hoping to find ancient documents which might help reconstruct the history of the Yucatán. On March 3rd, Chichén Itzá's highest pyramid came into view.

The first peculiarity of the site to attract their attention was the enormous "well" that opened wide near the temple ruins. This was an enormous natural karstic well that was typical of the area and different from the erosive formations they had seen thus far. These pools were the only water reserves that the Maya cities in this area of the Yucatán could turn to and they were the objects of worship. Sacrificial victims were thrown in here at regular intervals in honour of Chac, the god of rain and fertility.

ITURBIDE

Page 179 bottom – The ruins of Iturbide, the ancient city of Dzibilnocac: the structure drawn by Catherwood is today known as Building A-1.

CHICHÉN ITZÁ

Page 180 – The building known as Akab Dzib ("writing in the dark", because of the statue of a scribe located inside) at Chichén Itzá; the building dates from before the Toltec conquest.

Page 180 – Plan of the site of Chichén Itzá.

The name Chichén Itzá means "Well of the Itzá" and the city has a particularly interesting history. Between 800 and 950 AD, at the end of the Classic Period, when the Mayan cities on the lowlands had begun their decline and were being abandoned, a group of Maya peoples named Itzá, strongly influenced by the cultures of northern Mexico, founded a small centre linked to the cult of the Sacred Well. Then, at the end of the 10th century, the Toltecs arrived at Chichén Itzá. The invaders came from Tula, a city that had for many centuries dominated the Mexican highlands. The Toltecs introduced many aspects of the cruel Mexican religion into Mayan culture; they turned the city into a new capital and enriched it with majestic buildings. The Yucatán Maya were furthermore induced to worship the Plumed Serpent, a deity that here was

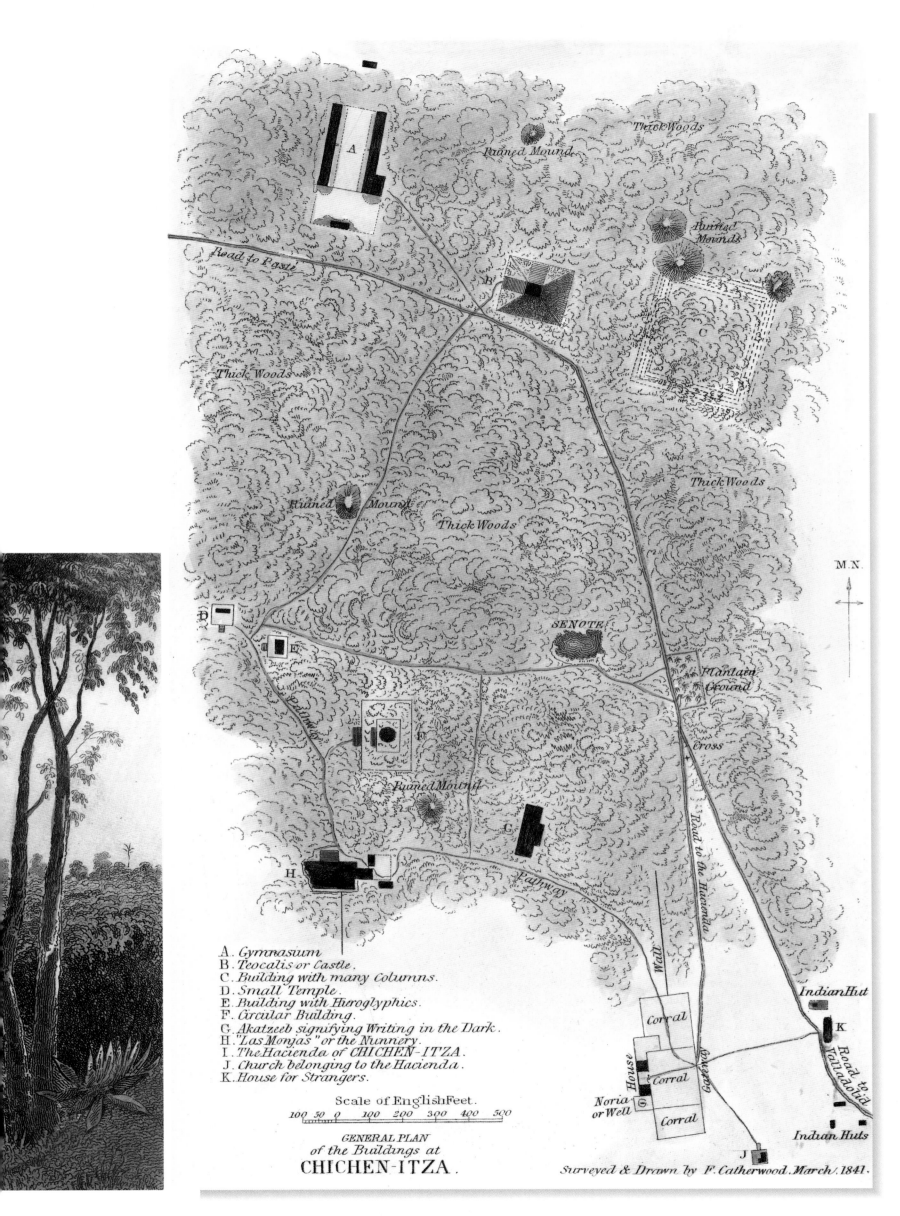

A. Gymnasium.
B. Teocalis or Castle.
C. Building with many Columns.
D. Small Temple.
E. Building with Hieroglyphics.
F. Circular Building.
G. Akatzeeb signifying Writing in the Dark.
H. "Las Monjas" or the Nunnery.
I. The Hacienda of CHICHEN-ITZA.
J. Church belonging to the Hacienda.
K. House for Strangers.

Scale of English Feet.
100 50 0 100 200 300 400 500

GENERAL PLAN
of the Buildings at
CHICHEN-ITZA.

Surveyed & Drawn by F. Catherwood. March. 1841.

called Kukulkán. Around 1000 AD, Chichén Itzá had already been transformed into a vast urban centre endowed with monuments attesting to the syncretism of the Mayan culture of the Late Classic Period with that of the Toltecs. The sculpture and decorations show the influence of a strongly militarised elite compared to those in the lowland cities that had flourished in previous centuries. The warring ideology that was a feature of Mesoamerican civilisations in the centuries immediately preceding the Spanish conquest is extremely evident here. Both Catherwood and Stephens, by then experts, realized that some determining event had occurred at Chichén Itzá, although they observed the same peculiar traits of the Mayan cultures, including the hieroglyphic inscriptions. The influence of the Puuc style is only seen in some of the buildings in the southern area of the site, of which the most important are the Coloured House, the Church and the Nunnery. The facade of the latter is entirely covered with stone fret designs and masks connected with the ancient cults of Chac and the Terrestrial Monster. On the other hand, there is a number of severely styled buildings from the Toltec period: the Castle (a nine-stepped pyramid topped by a magnificent temple), the Caracol (a surprising cylindrical building used as an astronomical observatory), the largest

CHICHÉN ITZÁ

Page 182-183 top – The small building attached to the so-called "Nunnery": it is a splendid example of pre-Toltec *Puuc* style.

Page 183 – The "Iglesia", a magnificent structure adjacent to the previous building, dates from the Late Classical period.

Pages 182-183 bottom – The three-storeyed building known as the Nunnery.

CHICHÉN ITZÁ

ball-court in America and the Temple of the Warriors flanked by the monumental Plaza of a Thousand Columns. The decline of Chichén Itzá came about in the 13th century when it was conquered and destroyed by the army of its great rival, Mayapán.

The three adventurers spent some of their most peaceful days at Chichén Itzá. They no longer suffered badly from malaria, the people in the nearby hacienda were friendly and the girls queued up to be photographed by Catherwood. Cabot, following his two vocations, divided his time between curing the sick and hunting birds. Frederick surveyed the ruins, drew the most beautiful monuments and reproduced the bas-reliefs that decorated some of the main buildings. He was also curious about the stone rings fixed in the walls of the ball-court through which the players used to pass the ball without touching it with their hands. He drew one decorated with the image of the Plumed Serpent. Stephens (who had guessed what the ball-court was used for) found a cycle of wall-paintings in a poor state of conservation in the Temple of the Jaguars but managed to make out the depiction of a naval battle.

Page 184 – Perhaps dating from the beginning of the Toltec period, the "Caracol" served as an observatory.

Pages 184-185 – One hundred and sixty-eight metres in length, the ball-court at Chichén Itzá is the largest in Meso-America.

Page 185 top – The two heads of the Plumed Serpent, placed at the bottom of the northern staircase of the "Castillo".

Page 185 bottom – The Castillo, an imposing square-based pyramid 30 metres in height, stands isolated in the great square of Chichén Itzá.

Page 186 – Detail of the wall-paintings that decorated the upper room of the Temple of the Jaguars; this building is attached to the ball-court.

Pages 186-187 – A section of the polychrome bas-reliefs that adorned the walls of the lower room in the Temple of the Jaguars.

Page 187 – Stone bas-reliefs situated on one of the jambs of the temple on the top of the Castillo at Chichén Itzá.

This part is covered with s

This part is covered with sculpture of the

Portion of a Painted Bas-relief on the Wall of a Building at CHICHE
Scale of English feet

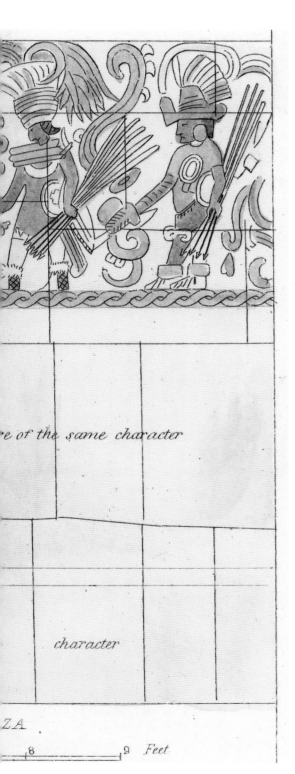

re of the same character

character

ZA

8   9 Feet

Pages 188-189 – The Temple of the Frescoes at Tulum, one of the last monuments biult by the Mayans before the Conquest.

Page 189 – The building opposite the Temple of the Frescoes at Tulum.

The expedition abandoned Chichén Itzá on 29 March 1842 and headed for the sea more than 125 miles away. First they stopped at Valladolid, a lovely Spanish city, then continued north-east. During the march, at Coba they were shown grave goods found in a Mayan tomb that Catherwood hurriedly drew. On 4 April, they arrived at the port of Yalahao where they went out in a punt to visit some islands – Contoy, Isla de las Muyeres and Cozumel – which were once inhabited by the Maya. They left Cozumel for Tulúm on the eastern coast of Yucatán.

Tulúm sits in an enchanting position on the top of a cliff; it was one of the last Mayan strongholds. The port and trading centre was built around 1200 AD and reached its zenith two centuries later following the fall of the city of Mayapán. Like other centres on the coast during the same period, Tulúm was originally surrounded by a defensive wall with lookout towers and walkways. It was also connected to the inland cities by raised roads. The city was inhabited when, in 1518, the Spanish led by Juan de Grijalva disembarked there.

Pages 190-191 – The so-called Temple
of the Falling God at Tulum.

Page 191 – View of the port of Yalahao,
now known as Chiquilà.

TULUM

At the time, the sanctuary consecrated to the goddess Ixchél on the island of Cozumel was a place of pilgrimage. Following the conquest, Tulúm was abandoned and fell into oblivion until the arrival of Stephens and Catherwood. As in the other coastal

influence exercised by Chichén Itzá. A second remarkable building, the Temple of the Frescoes, was built during the last years of the city. The inside walls are decorated with elegant paintings of mythological subjects, mainly in greys and blues, centring

centres, a mixture of Mayan and Mexican architectures is evident here. One of the main buildings is built right over the sea; this is the Castle, probably one of the oldest buildings in the city. The colonnade on the facade clearly shows the Mayan-Toltec

on an unidentified deity called the "Descending God", or the "Diver God", named for his posture. These frescoes strongly impressed Catherwood and Stephens who once again had their opinion of the greatness of Mayan art confirmed.

IZAMAL

Page 192 – The fascinating ruins of Aké, the remains of a Maya-Toltec temple.

Page 193 – The stucco mask that adorned the base of one of the great pyramids of Izamal.

Once they had returned to Yalahao, Stephens, Catherwood and Cabot sailed direct to the port of Silan from where they continued overland to the inland town of Izamal. Here they were shown the majestic ruin of Aké decorated on one side by a large stucco mask that Catherwood wanted to draw. Then, leaving Aké behind

built by the Egyptians or other peoples that had arrived by sea, nor that they were as old as had been supposed. Their estimates were surprisingly close to historical facts: they believed the oldest centres were founded around the 5th century and the most recent no earlier than the 13th century.

On May 18, they sailed to Sisal

them, they headed for the familiar town of Mérida.

It was time to return home. They had brought more than forty Mayan cities back from the oblivion of the centuries and the expedition could be counted a tremendous success despite the exhaustion and malaria. Stephens and Catherwood could now demonstrate without doubt that the cities of Central America had not been

to then continue to Cuba where they arrived two weeks later and spent several days admiring the local beauties. They were given a little trouble when it was time to pass their graphic materials, plaster casts, archaeological finds and the hundreds of birds stuffed by Cabot through Customs, but in the end, Stephens' diplomacy prevailed and on 4 June they were once more at sea.

FAME AND GLORY

The trio set foot back in New York on 17 June 1842 and were immediately occupied by frenetic activity. Cabot spent some months organising the first ornithological collection ever dedicated to Central America, then returned to medicine. Later he was to become one of the most highly considered surgeons in the United States. Stephens and Catherwood were welcomed triumphantly and set out their objects in the Rotonda on Prince Street. The residents of New York queued to admire the carved wood architraves, the sculptures, the panels and bas-reliefs discovered in the Mayan cities. For the first time, the public was able to see first hand the unique artistic forms, to admire the faces of the unknown Mayan rulers and to contemplate the friezes and bizarrely - shaped ornaments that were clearly outside the canons of classical art.

It was a triumph, but it only lasted a short time. In the evening of 31 July 1842, the Rotonda caught fire and quickly turned into a blaze. In just a few minutes, much of Frederick Catherwood's life's work was destroyed. The huge panoramas, the drawings made in such difficult circumstances in Central America, the plans of the cities and Mayan monuments, the daguerreotypes and all the valuable objects he had brought back from the Yucatán — all went up in flames. This was a disaster of incalculable proportions, and not just financial. The causes of the fire remain unknown: maybe the negligence of a janitor, pure chance or a criminal act by some deranged individual. What was important was that an extraordinary archaeological patrimony had been irredeemably lost. It was, of course, a huge blow to Stephens. To soothe the pain, the two could only throw themselves into a fit of activity that absorbed all their emotional resources.

On 7 December 1842, with many other people of importance, Stephens and Catherwood were founding members of the American Ethnological Society. Then, besieged by admirers and spurred on by the Harper brothers, Stephens sat down to write his new adventure. This time, an extensive bibliographical research of ancient texts was required as Stephens had set himself the task of proving beyond reasonable doubt that the Maya culture was absolutely original. For his part, Catherwood gathered all the material that was left to him and began to produce the illustrations for Stephens' book. Luckily, as soon as he had returned to New York, he had delivered many of his drawings to Harper Bros. so that the editors had an idea of how much they had discovered in the Yucatán, while his notes and sketches were held safe at his house. There was, therefore, sufficient material and once again he was entirely responsible for the graphical work. Incidents of Travel in Yucatan, published in two volumes and illustrated with one hundred and twenty lithographs, appeared in bookshops in record time. In March 1843, thousands of readers were able to pore avidly over the gripping story of the trip as described by the brilliant explorer. Once more, the book was a success and was reprinted until as late as 1865. It was also translated into many languages and it fascinated generations of readers around half the world who boggled at the pictures as they dreamed of being among the forests and ruins of Yucatán.

On the crest of their success, the two dreamed up an extremely ambitious project, the publication of a large work in four volumes entirely dedicated to the antiquities of Mesoamerica and illustrated with one hundred and twenty colour lithographs. The text would be the responsibility of Stephens with contributions from the celebrated ornithologist Albert Gallatin, the geographer Alexander von Humboldt, the Egyptologist Sir John Wilkinson, and the historian William Prescott. All were famous names from the world of culture of the period. To cover the huge costs of such a work, it was necessary to find at least nine hundred subscribers, so the help of the New York Historical

Society was requested and promptly given. The omens were encouraging: Stephens and Catherwood enjoyed the unconditional esteem of the American academic world and the preparatory water-colours were unanimously deemed splendid, but the thing did not work. The required number of subscribers could not be found — perhaps because of the cost of the work, 100 dollars, which was extremely high for the time — and soon Harper Bros. withdrew from the project. Even Stephens, profoundly demoralised, lost interest and let the idea founder despite the booksellers Bartlett and Welford offering to uphold the initiative. At that point, Catherwood decided to go ahead alone and it is due to his determination alone that we can today still admire what must be considered the greatest artistic presentation of Mayan art ever produced. As nobody in America was prepared to offer him concrete assistance, he sailed to London with his entire family in July 1843 where he installed them in his paternal home as the guests of his brother Alfred. But even here he was unable to convince any editor of the potential of his project. After traipsing around all the offices, all he received were refusals made all the more bitter by the fact that Stephens had, for some unknown reason, refused to help in any way. Such behaviour is extremely perplexing considering the friendship between the two men. Nonetheless, all the more resolved not to let himself be mocked by fate for the umpteenth time, Frederick did not give in. It was time to publish at least some of his efforts. So, as he wrote in a letter to William Prescott, a fervent admirer, he took the decision to "become my own editor".

Despite the serious economic blow he had suffered, he still had enough financial resources to continue. He convened six of the best English engravers so that they could lithograph the drawings he had chosen as the most representative of the art and architecture of the Maya. He chose Owen Jones, an old friend, to print them. Distributors of the book in the United States were to be Bartlett and Welford, the only ones to have shown faith in his capabilities. The project cost him just over 307 pounds, a notable sum, and the edition was limited to three hundred copies. Of these, only a few (the number is unknown) appeared in the luxury edition with plates hand coloured by Catherwood. Views of Ancient Monuments in Central America, Chiapas and Yucatan — dedicated to John Stephens — appeared to the public in May 1844 and was received as a masterpiece. It was divided into two volumes, had a frontispiece by Owen Jones, an accurate, three colour map of Central America and twenty six plates printed on twenty five sheets. The introduction and comments on each illustration were written by Catherwood who showed himself also to be a reasonable writer; his prose was not of the best style but it was articulate and filled with precise observations. The opinions expressed by Catherwood that the ancient peoples of Central America were to be considered indigenous and the creators of original artistic forms that showed "but very slight and accidental analogies with the works of any people or country in the Old World" turned out to be correct and are still considered so. His writings and the lectures he gave after publication of the book contributed in a conclusive manner to the birth of a new school of thought, one that is now universally accepted. At forty five years of age, and finally out of the shadow of the brilliant, charismatic and exuberant John Stephens, "Mr Catherwood" had finally achieved the fame and regard he had deserved for a very long time.

Pages 194-195 — Plate XII (depicting the Castillo of Chichén Itzá) and a detail of the same plate, taken from the standard edition of *Views of Ancient Monuments of Central America, Chiapas and Yucatan*. In order to create his masterpiece, Catherwood had lithographs made of the drawings of six of the leading English engravers of the period: J.C. Bourne, G. Moore, W. Parrott, A. Picken, T. Scotter Boys, H. Warren.

THE SAD EPILOGUE TO AN ADVENTUROUS LIFE

Unfortunately, fame and regard are not everything. Even if Views of Ancient Monuments *sold well, the money he earned was not enough to keep his family. Frederick enjoyed enormous prestige in the field of art and archaeology and Londoners fought to be able to attend the lectures of such a popular person but once more he was troubled by money problems. So he decided to return to his previous profession, architecture or civil engineering. With hindsight, this was a tragic turnaround, a grave loss to the history of art and pre-Columbian civilisations. William Prescott had suggested that Catherwood turn his attention to Peru and the mysterious civilisations that had been ruthlessly destroyed by Francisco Pizarro and his gang of bloodthirsty adventurers in the 16th century. If only the Panorama had not been burned to the ground! Catherwood would then not have found himself in financial straits worrying about his children's education, and he would have been able to follow his friend's advice and his own explorative spirit. But it was not to be and we can never regret our loss enough.*

After a brief experience during the construction of the railway that linked Sheffield to Manchester, Catherwood returned to Prince Street in New York with his family in August 1844

intending to design houses for rich members of the middle class. In the meantime he exhibited some paintings taken from drawings made in Central America and entered tenders for the construction of a fountain and a monument to George Washington, but without success. He painted a famous View of New York from Governors Island in this period. In April 1845 he unexpectedly published a report on the monuments of Dougga which he had visited twelve years before.

After returning to London in autumn 1845, he was called by the Demerara Railway Company which had been formed to build a railway line in British Guiana to transport local produce to the coast. After a first on-site inspection at the end of 1845 and in early 1846 (which also took him to Jamaica and the United States to inspect other railways), Frederick was confirmed project manager and works supervisor in April 1847. Proof that he had now abandoned his past life as explorer, scholar and artist is given by the fact that in 1846 he was contacted by Professor James Fergusson, a famous art historian, who argued that Omar's Mosque in Jerusalem had not been built by the Arabs at the turn of the 7th century, but by the Emperor Constantine nearly four hundred years earlier over Christ's tomb, and that therefore it was this monument that should be

Pages 196-197 – This "View of New York" seen from Governor's Island, executed in 1844, is one of the last paintings executed by Frederick Catherwood.

Page 199 – Plate XI of the standard edition of the *Views of Ancient Monuments*, depicting the temple on the top of the Pyramid of the Magician at Uxmal.

considered the Holy Sepulchre. To strengthen his hypothesis – later shown to be fallacious – the famous English scholar asked Catherwood to provide him with his entire artistic documentation produced in 1834 and never published despite its outstanding documentary value. In January 1847, Catherwood obliged and, in doing so,

set to building the first railway in South America. Unfortunately, the site was ravaged by incidents and delays of every kind, and to make matters worse, Catherwood was struck down by violent attacks of malaria as a result of the unhealthy climate. Devastated by his continual bouts of fever, beset by thousands of problems

supported the political theories of Thomas Jefferson in 1792, then carried forward by Andrew Jackson. It was the purpose of politics to put into practice the rights of man and to bring equality to society through defence of constitutional liberties and the autonomy of the states. Consequently, Catherwood had never come into contact with aristocrats, rich industrialists, bankers and the privileged in general. His libertarian spirit, made caustic by the illness, rendered him irascible, bitter and aggressive to the local estate owners and shareholders of the Demerara Railway Company, though they held his irreproachable professionalism in high regard. In short, relations grew insupportable and in 1849 the contract was cancelled. Catherwood returned to London where fate once more put him in contact with Stephens. During the period since they were last together, Stephens had become one of the founders of the Hudson River Rail-line company and in 1847 director of a shipping company, the Ocean Steam Navigation Company. The New York lawyer had also turned his back on archaeology, preferring to invest his money in profitable speculations that were also to confer fame and respect on him. But his interest in science was still strong and when he went to Germany on a business trip, he had wanted to meet the great geographer, Alexander von Humboldt, in person.

convinced his friend Arundale to do the same. Fergusson never returned the drawings and they have never been seen since.

Around the middle of 1847, Frederick returned to British Guiana where he was warmly welcomed and

(including the termites that were eating the sleepers), and debilitated by the steamy heat of the jungle, his character worsened day by day and likewise his relationship with his clients. Above all, Frederick was a convinced democrat if not a radical; in America, he had fully

In 1848, Stephens had founded the Panama Railroad Company with two wealthy partners. It was their plan to succeed where so many attempts had failed over the past decades in connecting the Atlantic and Pacific oceans via a much-needed railway line across the Isthmus of Panama.

California had just become the promised land and American entrepreneurs and fortune-hunters wanted a way to get there as quickly as possible. Stephens' railway was the solution to their problems. The difficulties to overcome were frightening, and not only of a technical nature, as the interests involved were enormous; both France and Great Britain were hostile to Washington's supremacy in the area but in the end Stephens succeeded in his intent. The success, once more, owed much to Catherwood who had, after some pressure, accepted responsibility for the works though the pay was not exceptional. As usual suffering from financial problems, Frederick left the family home in Hoxton in January 1850. He had been asked to write a book on the Maya but he had refused as he did not feel up to the task as a writer. Working in Panama was another risk to a man whose health had been undermined by malaria and, before long, he would have to deal with thousands of desperate men wanting to head for California where "gold fever" was rising quickly. Catherwood and Stephens embraced once more in a miserable village on the Atlantic coast, then the American had to leave for Bogotà where he was required to look after the interests of the company.

The climate in Panama was infernal, hot and humid beyond all endurance, and the jungle was infested with every sort of insect, most of them harmful. Taken by the thought of easy earnings in California, the workers that were engaged to build the railway worked with all haste while the new arrivals fell ill one after another. Catherwood performed a true miracle: not only did he manage to take the works forward, he also cured crowds of feverish patients, heartened those

with broken spirits and gave a dignified burial to the unfortunate, of which there were too many.

Stephens' health meanwhile was worsening day by day; from Bogotà he had to return to convalesce in New York where he was elected President of the Panama Railway Company. He had not been able to meet his old friend, nor reassure him of the future which to Catherwood seemed ever blacker. Once his contract with the railway company expired without the guarantee of a renewal or recompense for the extra work he had put in, he also decided to try his luck in California. He did not know that the section of railway that he had succeeded in building had saved the

company from bankruptcy. The aspiring gold-seekers had paid dearly to put down the few miles of track from Limón towards Panama City and the Pacific, and the income generated was used to finance the next part of the works, concluded in 1855. While Catherwood was leaving to search for gold, Stephens, suffering from malaria, returned to Panama to check the state of the site and to accelerate the final phase of the massive project. This trip was to be his last.

In August 1850, meanwhile, Catherwood had disembarked at San Francisco, a city in rapid expansion where, like New York fourteen years earlier, they were rebuilding the houses destroyed after a recent fire. When he had supplemented his exhausted finances, he went to Oregon to carry out a topographical survey of the valley of the river Willamette where

colonies were to be built. He then went back to plan the railway from Benecia (today a suburb of San Francisco) to Marysville. The pay was good, the climate ideal and, for once, "Mr Catherwood" was satisfied. He had even taken American nationality as California had become the 31st state of the US on 9 September 1850 and, in doing so, everyone living there had automatically received nationality. As usual, the good news did not last long. In June 1851, having lost a large amount of money in a bad investment, he decided to return once more to London. He set sail for Panama where, ironically, he travelled over the section of railway he had put so much effort into and for which he had received so little. Here he met Stephens for the last time. The American's health was by now utterly ruined but they spoke of recently discovered remains they had heard of in southern California. After this reunion, Catherwood continued on his way to his native England. Stephens had left New York against the advice of his doctors, supported by his unsinkable belief in himself and by the enthusiasm that had guided him in the deserts of Arabia Petrea and the jungles of Guatemala, but belief and enthusiasm were not enough in the fetid forests of Panama. One day he collapsed to the ground at the foot of a tree he was particularly fond of. After receiving initial treatment, he was put on board a boat for New York but it was already too late. Malaria had eaten away at him for years destroying his liver and kidneys and hepatitis had overcome his final resistance. John Lloyd Stephens died on 13 October 1852 at the age of forty seven.

An obituary in the Putnam's Monthly Magazine was written by the Reverend Francis Lister Hawks, rector of St. Thomas's Episcopal church in New York; in it, Hawks said that he had met Stephens in London in 1836 at the time when the American was writing children's books for Harper Bros. and that it was Hawks himself who encouraged Stephens to take up a career in writing. The brilliant results of this encouragement still enthral readers around the world as the three books Incidents of Travel, are

obviously, the wish remained a dream. In September 1852 he was once more in California where he worked with alacrity on the Marysville railway project until April 1853. He then returned to London where he wanted at all costs to oversee the English reprint of Incidents of Travel in Central America, published in 1854 by Arthur Hall, Virtue & Co., to which

which now covered Manhattan. Having departed from Liverpool with 385 passengers on board, the steamship SS Arctic was rammed by the French steamer Vesta off Newfoundland on 27 September 1854. The captain and many of the crew filled the few lifeboats and survived, but almost all the passengers were left to fend for themselves and they died miserably in the freezing waters of the

periodically reprinted.

Catherwood was ignorant of his friend's death and wrote him a letter, today conserved at the Bankroft Library at the University of California, in which he explained his plans for the future. He told of his involvement in a mining company in California and of his ambitious desire to explore the ruins they had spoken of in Panama. He longed to undertake another expedition and make new lithographs to be added as an appendix to Stephens' books but,

he added eight new engravings and the portrait of Stephens. Frederick also wrote a short introduction to the work in which he gave a short but accurate description of his friend. In September of the same year he made his umpteenth journey to New York to check in person how the Benecia-Marysville Railroad and Gold Hill companies were doing (Gold Hill was the mining company in which he had invested a good part of his savings) but he never saw the forest of buildings

Atlantic. The news of the terrible disaster reached New York two weeks later with the list of the dead. In a mocking twist of fate, one name was missing — an oversight that smacks of incredible. Frederick's death was only verified after many days and at the insistence of Stephens' family.

"Mr Catherwood", architect, Egyptologist, artist, surveyor, painter, pioneer of Mesoamerican archaeology and railway builder, had passed away unnoticed, just as he had spent most of his extraordinary life.